Awakening

A 40-Day Journey toward Deeper Intimacy with God

John & Shannon Boyd

FORGE

Kingdom Building Ministries

Awakening: A 40-Day Journey toward Deeper Intimacy with God

Forge

ISBN No. 9780978814267

Published by Forge,
14485 E. Evans Ave., Denver, Colorado 80014

Unless otherwise stated, Scripture quotations are taken from the Holy Bible, New International Version® NIV® Copyright © 1973,1978, 1984 by International Bible Society. Used by permission of Zondervan. All rights reserved.

Requests to use material contained in this publication should be sent in writing to: Publisher, Forge 14485 E. Evans Ave., Denver, CO 80014

Written by John and Shannon Boyd
Back cover Photograph by Maggie Boyd

Visit us online at www.forgeforward.org

For Maggie, Audrey, and Aidan —

Thank you for helping us to discover
the mysteries of God
in everyday places and spaces.

TABLE OF CONTENTS

Foreword

Over a period of many years I read biographies of great men and women of God. Their stories enthralled me. Colorfully woven within the greater tapestry of God's story of love, common themes began to emerge from the accounts of their lives: humble beginnings, great odds against them, hardships and challenges, enduring faith, steady obedience, and the revelation that in spite of how very ordinary these individuals were, they established huge legacies beyond earthly life spans. The impact of their faith and obedience spread far and wide to people and landscapes beyond their own time and space, leaving never-to-be-forgotten lasting imprints on the world.

The more I read, one common and crucial thread seemed to emerge from these faithful yet quite diverse God followers from all around the world: these people who did great things for God were people who loved God greatly. Their authentic and passionate love relationship with Him transformed their ordinary lives to people of extraordinary worth and fruitfulness to God's Kingdom.

These faith-full, faith-forward, Kingdom laboring servants whose hearts were marked by love, didn't merely talk about God—they actually knew Him. They communed with Him. They had tasted His love, experienced His goodness, and their hungry hearts wanted more of Him, His will, His Word, and His glory. They took to heart what Jesus said matters most—loving God with all of their heart, mind, soul, and strength. Their lives demonstrated their conviction, and they made loving God the main thing in their lives.

They revealed through their exemplary lives of love that the greatest gift we can offer the world is an intense, real, and focused love for God. A life of ongoing, cultivated intimacy with God brings Him to the everyday scenes of our lives and to the people we and God love deeply. An intimate love relationship with God is vastly different than a life of doing things for God. Knowing great things about God pales in light of actually knowing Him and walking with Him. The faithful ones of God made "more of God, more of His will, and more of His glory" their offering, and the world has never been the same.

Will you and I offer less than God's highest and best—the overflow of a life that has been with Jesus, fully awakened and alive in Him?

The opportunity discovered by generations past is yet alive and available for you! Will you leave a legacy of love that flows from being in love with God? Will you allow His heart to awaken yours? Will you lean into God more than you ever have as He asks, "Will you draw close to me" (Jeremiah 30:21)? Will you trust Him and let Him lead you as you read, write, reflect, and respond through His "awakening" words and presence? Will you approach God with a humble and teachable spirit? Will you express your vulnerabilities and insecurities to Him? Will you take Him up on His invitation to spend forty days of intimate, up-close, and deep-down communion with Him?

This world may be waiting for your awakened soul, your revitalized connection, your heart of love connected with a living and loving God. There are people around you who need and want more of God—His presence, love, kindness, hope, mercy, justice, and peace. Your life up-close and intimate with God might be the awakening catalyst they need to experience the extravagant love and grace of God. Through you, God is ready to do great things. Are you ready to love Him greatly?

Dwight Robertson
Founding President of Forge
Author of *You are God's Plan A*

Introduction

So you want to fall in love with God? Maybe you've really never thought of your relationship with God in those terms, but if you picked up this book and started reading, there's a good chance that's exactly what you're after. If so, you're not alone. It doesn't matter how rugged your skin, tough your interior, or poetic and tender your soul—if you are breathing, you were made for deep and abiding love. While our lives are as unique as our fingerprints, we are all part of a much larger story that runs steady and true. "You were made for God alone," the great theologian, Augustine, once said, "and you will not find rest, until you find your rest in him." Written deep within the plot of each of our stories is a desire to love and be loved by the One who first loved us. We can deny it, run from it, argue against it, or try to manage it; but if we allow our souls to be quiet long enough to really listen, we know it's true. We want to experience true love in its fullest capacity. And that means falling in love with God, the author of all love and faith, including ours.

While you may not know exactly how to go about loving God more intimately, like a dormant seed buried beneath the winter snow, you most likely sense that you were meant for something more than what you currently have and are. Somewhere along the line, you may have believed the subtle lie that this love isn't for someone like you. Perhaps you're one who has been hurt by someone who didn't tend love well and now you're "once bitten, twice shy." Maybe love at some point became too painful and costly and you pushed it down, back, or to the side. Perhaps you were sold a lesser version of love by well-meaning but broken people, pastors, parents, or _____ (you fill in the blank) that came with all kinds of strings attached and hoops to jump through. Is it possible that you've never really seen what genuine, unadulterated, grace-filled, and lavishly beautiful love looks like ... but if you saw it, you'd surely want it?

Certainly, something within you longs for more—more of God, more of His love, more of His plans and purposes, and more of His glory being put on display in your life and in the world. Maybe it's time to till some soil, shed some lies, and open your heart as never before to the God who bids you to come.

Are you ready to respond to God's loving invitation to "arise, my love, my beautiful one, and come with me" (Song of Songs 2:10) ?

A Few Pre-Journey Thoughts

This experience will not "fix" you, but it will guide you.

If you're looking for a book on "Ten Steps to a Better Relationship with God," you'll most likely be disappointed by this resource or any other that over-promises and under-delivers. Falling in love with God or anyone else is not something you can program, strategize or check off. Love doesn't work that way. Love isn't a "thing" to be handled but something alive to be stewarded and nurtured. Love is as natural as taking a breath. Like a deer panting for water (Psalm 42:1), love is as instinctual as flowers, trees, puppies, and children that seem to grow up all on their own (Mark 4:26-29). We can't "make" love grow. But we can turn our hearts toward the sun. We can create the right environment for love to sprout, blossom, and mature. While this experience won't "fix" you, it will help you to better posture your heart toward God so that your love can deepen and bear fruit.

This experience comes with cost and risk.

Love is a risky business. To love much, we must risk much. "Putting ourselves out there" always has the potential of hurt and pain. Far too often we have seen and even experienced "love gone bad," where we have felt kicked to the curb, misunderstood, rejected, and left alone to lick our wounds. That's understandable. Unfortunately, as marred human beings, our broken ways of loving often create such scenarios. But God's love is not like that. While others don't tend our hearts well, God always does. Still, giving our heart to God isn't easy. We have to let go of control, expectations, self-centered motives and desires, awkwardness, and pride. We have to risk handing God "all that we have and all that we are" and trust that He will steward our love well.

The question is often asked, "How far can I go in this love relationship with God?" Perhaps the better question is, "How much of your life are you willing to give to Him?"

This experience is a love adventure in process.

Love isn't a contract to be signed but an ongoing adventure to be lived. Your love adventure is a magnificent story written in many chapters with all kinds of twists, turns, discoveries, and challenges. It will take time for the story to unfold, for the plot to make sense and for themes to develop. It will require patience on your part. You will have to trust God, the author, in this. God won't just plop love into your heart. But in His time and for His purposes, as you continue to trust Him, He will look after your heart, deepen your love, and write your story magnificently well.

This experience is part of a greater love story being written.

The story of love that God is writing in you is not for you alone. You are a part of a much bigger story in the making. The gospel writer, John, tells us that it is the "world" that God loves so much (John 3:16). God wants all people, everywhere and anywhere, to know the depths of His love and enjoy Him forever. Your story fits perfectly into God's bigger story that begins and ends with an unchanging, always and forever, love.

Although God's love has remained faithful and true, ours has not. Still, all of our running, hiding, and rebelling hasn't changed God's opinion of us one bit. He continues to love us with an everlasting love.

God's story of redeeming and restoring love is meant to be written in you and through you. The more in love with God we become, the more our story collides with His larger love story. There, we and others find life and God is put on display.

As you travel these next forty days, know that God is not interested in your goodness as much as He is your heart. His greatest desire is that you long to love and please Him. May your time with Him help you to "grasp just how wide and long and high and deep is his love … that you may be filled to the measure of the fullness of God" (Ephesians 3:18-19).

How to Use This Guide

This 40-day experience is designed to both help you encounter and experience God in deeper ways and to help you establish healthy practices and rhythms that will give your love relationship with God the right kind of environment in which to grow and mature.

Forty Days/Four Movements

There is nothing magical or exclusive about the length of this experience or the format of each day. Through the centuries, many faithful followers of Christ have laid out spiritual disciplines and practices that have been helpful in encountering God and growing in faith and love. The experience that Awakening invites you to is just that: an experience. Our hope is that through our writing and God's inviting, you will find new spaces and places for God to meet you.

The thought behind forty days is two-fold. One, on a practical note, research shows that when we create habits and rhythms for thirty days, we are more likely to continue those practices. So, if thirty days will do the trick, then forty days might just be that much better. We want to do whatever we can to help your love relationship with God thrive! Two, and a bit more on the spiritual side, forty days is the length of time Jesus spent in the wilderness in intimate time with the Father. There, His love was put to the test. There, His love grew as He leaned into and upon His Father. There, the greatest gift He would offer the world was being shaped and strengthened through His intimacy with God. As you journey with God over the next forty days, our hope for you is the same.

About the four daily movements. When we engage any significant conversation in life, a very basic pattern takes place. Whether conversing with a friend, spouse, family member, co-worker or neighbor we follow a four-step process or movement: we position ourselves to best hear and be heard; we communicate about whatever subject is at hand; we respond to what was said in some form or fashion; and we conclude the conversation with a goodbye.

That same kind of healthy communication takes place in our conversations and communications with God. Because God is God (and we are not), the four movements of conversation look a little different for us than they do for Him. Still, the principles of good communication remain the same as we give God our full attention; listen to what He has to say; respond to whatever He's communicated; and receive His blessing as we go.

11

For simplicity, we will call these four movements of encountering God: Re-position, Renew, Respond and Receive. The beauty of these movements is that they help us to engage in meaningful five minute encounters with God in the same manner that we might find meaning in a fifty minute or five hour exchange with Him. While these four movements are by no means the only way to approach God, we have found them to help create space for intimate encounters and conversations to take place with Him.

Re-position: ◁▷

Activity, noise, and distraction fill the bulk of our lives. Life gets so loud we can barely hear ourselves think, let alone hear what God is saying. Jesus often withdrew to out-of-the-way places for undistracted time with God (Luke 5:16, The Message). Shifting from chaos to solitude takes some re-positioning of body, mind, and spirit.

Re-positioning helps us to break away from whatever is otherwise holding our attention so that we may give ourselves more fully to God. It's much like the response to an African greeting in the Tswana language. "Where are you?" says the greeter. "I am here," comes the response, "I am fully present." Re-positioning is about saying to God in any given moment, "I am here, Lord. You have my full attention."

Renew: ✝

To spend time with God is to invite His transformation. "Be transformed," Paul tells us, "by the renewing of your mind" (Romans 12:2). God thinks too highly of us not to cultivate in us the love that He planted. As we give God our full attention, He lovingly encourages, challenges, refines, builds up, moves forward, convinces, convicts, leads, disciplines, instructs, points out, cheers up, cheers on … and a thousand and one other things that makes us more fully alive as human beings and more fruitful as laborers in His Kingdom. Whether through the Scriptures (where God promises to always speak) or through another means of communication of His own choosing, God wants to take us deeper into his love and fellowship—step by step, conversation by conversation, encounter by encounter.

Respond:

We can't be in God's presence and not respond. His action calls for our re-action. Responding to God calls for a commitment from us and keeps us from just talking a good game when it comes to our relationship with Jesus and others. Love puts its money where its mouth is. Our response to being in God's presence may come in the form of thanksgiving, commitment, listening, reflection, praise, prayer, or action. No matter the form, when God speaks, acts, and renews—we must respond.

Receive:

We end our time together by receiving from God a gift of Himself. As in any loving encounter, God wants to send us on our way with a goodbye kiss, a firm embrace, an encouraging word, or an affirming proclamation. God wants His blessing and favor to penetrate our mind, stir our heart, and engage our will. As we leave, we openly receive God's gifts—grace, mercy, peace, power, provision, presence, and so much more—as we remember His promise to be with us "always" (Matthew 28:20).

How to daily engage in this experience

This travel guide is intended to free you, not constrain you. The daily readings and exercises are prayerfully thought-out guides to lead you in your 40-day experience with God. While this traveling resource seeks to help you find the space and assistance necessary to deepen your intimacy with God, our hope and prayer is that God, and not this guide, is the one who leads you.

The daily readings and exercises are fairly self-explanatory. While there is some space provided to write and reflect, you may want to use a notebook or a journal as well. Whatever you think will help you to continue intimate habits with God will work best. Bringing along your Bible is always a good idea. Most of the Scriptures needed for the daily encounters are printed out for you, but God might direct you elsewhere as you go—so, it is best to be prepared. While this experience is designed to be journeyed in forty days, missing a day here and there is perfectly okay. Just pick up where you left off.

Be well assured that as you put your whole heart, mind, and soul into this exercise that God will meet you in significant ways far beyond the pages of this guide. "When you seek Me with your whole heart," God promises, "you will find Me." Let it be so.

Traveling Tips as You Begin Your Journey

- Know that God wants to meet you honestly and authentically wherever you are—whether at your worst or best. This is the place to let down your guard and trust that more than anything, God really loves you, is awfully fond of you, and has your very best interest in mind.

- This is not an exercise to be checked off but an encounter with God to be experienced! Don't concern yourself with getting it all in or doing it right as much as positioning yourself to receive whatever God desires in your time together.

- God knows how you are wired (how you think, feel, and understand) … trust Him to meet you in a way that connects with the unique way He designed you. If you seek Him with your whole heart, you won't miss a thing He has for you. Take on the posture of Samuel, "Speak, Lord, your servant is listening" (I Samuel 3:10).

- Resist minding the clock. Make your focus God's presence. It's okay for silence and spaces of inactivity to do their work. Whether listening, reading, walking, or writing, know that God simply wants to be with you in all of it.

- Don't have an agenda other than God's. It's fine to have a plan. We think the one we provided is actually a pretty good one. Just be open to having it altered. Don't anticipate, participate. Set aside expectations of what you will hear, feel, experience, or learn. Be attentive to God's movement in and around you … and relax. Leave the results to God.

WEEK 1
God's Love Story

In the beginning there was God,
and if you really knew Him, you would love Him.
God not only created the world, He created you,
and He actually delights in knowing you
and desires for you to know Him.
He's compassionate and gracious, slow to anger,
and abounding in love and faithfulness.
Most of all, God is love.
And out of His love He says to you, "Come,
make your home in Me, and I will make My home in you."

DAY 1
A GOD WHO INVITES YOU

Today is the beginning of a beautiful journey with Jesus. You may feel a little awkward as you begin this trip. Perhaps it feels a bit like the first day at a new school or job. Everything around you may seem unfamiliar, and the prospect of getting to know Jesus in the way you had once hoped suddenly seems like a far off venture out of your grasp. If that's the state of your heart and mind today, relax. You're on the right bus and heading in the right direction. Jesus is as easy a traveling companion as they come. So, if necessary, let discomfort have its way for a day or two. Soon enough, the awkward will fade as Jesus' voice and face becomes more and more familiar. For now, trust the process, follow the signs and be open and honest with Jesus. He's already aware of your given state. He's ready to meet you right where you are.

RE-POSITION

Hopefully you're in a place and space that you feel free to unwind and let go of some things. Take a few minutes simply to rest in God's presence. Close your eyes and become aware of your breathing and the One who gave you breath. Allow the tension in your body to slowly be released. Relax in God's presence as you picture Him with you—because He is.

Let Him know you are here to meet Him. As if He were sitting across from you, take a minute or two to tell Him why you're here today, why you're on this journey, and what you hope comes from traveling with Him these forty days.

RENEW

God's word is active and living and true. It can be trusted. Read the following verse slowly and carefully. Read it through two or three times. After each reading, pause—let God's Word wash over your heart and mind. Listen for your traveling companion, Jesus. If you don't hear anything, it's okay. God won't let you miss anything He wants you to hear.

Then Jesus said, "Come to me, all of you who are weary and carry heavy burdens, and I will give you rest."
(Matthew 11:28)

In the space below, write down anything you heard God say or even thought you might have heard Him say. If it's a picture, perhaps draw it. Don't dismiss things as unimportant, and say to yourself, "that's probably my voice and not God's." Be assured that, in time, God's voice will become more recognizable.

FOOD FOR THOUGHT AND REFLECTION

There are not many among us who are not weary, who do not carry heavy burdens. The world weighs a lot, and so often we frantically try to carry it. Whether the suitcase we lug around holds our own struggles and feelings of unworthiness or it holds the various pains and anxieties of others or every combination in between, we were not created to live in the unrest and the overwhelming fatigue that comes from being weighed down.

Jesus says, "Come."

Tenderly, the invitation proceeds from the heart of Christ. No condemnation. No prerequisite. No step-by-step.

If you're weary, come to Me.
If you're carrying heavy burdens, come to Me.
Come to Me. I'll give you rest.

What does it look like to enter into the rest Christ offers, to learn from Him? Sometimes the first encounters seem strange. Sometimes we resist, because we tell ourselves that we're doing just fine on our own. And it seems strange. So we wait, wearier and heavier laden. And still Jesus beckons.

Come to Me, I will give you rest.

Perhaps a place to begin to learn from Christ is to take Him up on the invitation, to lay down arms and suitcases and pride and feelings of unworthiness. He invites us. The God who formed you and gave you breath and life is asking you to come to Him. What if we just entered in? What if we released the grip on the handle of control, and we just accepted the invitation God is extending?

RESPOND

Most of us travel with way too much baggage. What is some of yours? As you begin this journey, tell Jesus as honestly as possible about some of the junk you carry that might make this trip burdensome. Offer these things to Jesus and ask Him to kindly take them from you.

God has invited you to a journey and a conversation. What will you do with it? What will you write to God on your R.S.V.P.?

RECEIVE

As your journey begins, go with this blessing. Insert your name below and listen as Jesus says in a very personal way …

_____, I will bless you and keep you; my face is forever shining toward you. My grace is upon you. My peace is here. (Numbers 6:24-26)

DAY 2
A GOD WHO FIRST LOVED YOU

A new day, with new mercies, and a new opportunity to take in the unfathomable reality that "I am my beloved's and He is mine" — all made possible because of a God who loved and has taken notice of us, first.

RE-POSITION

As in Day 1, take some time to simply breathe. Become aware of God by becoming more aware of the fact that you are actually living and breathing, and that He's the one who has given you breath.

Try this: when you inhale, take in the presence of the Holy Spirit. Allow His life to fill not only your lungs but also your mind and your soul. When you exhale, let stale and used up air exit your body along with any distraction, burden, frustration, sin, confusion, weariness, etc. The idea is to take in the life God gives and release from your being anything that is not life-giving. No need to rush here. This could be the most important place you encounter God today.

RENEW

The following verse is profoundly simple and true. Read this verse carefully and intentionally seven times, each time putting the emphasis on a different word. For instance, the first time through, read it this way, "WE love because he first loved us." The second time, this way, "We LOVE because …" and so on. Each time you read through the verse and emphasize a different word, pause. Allow thoughts, questions, and feelings to flow. Whatever you are hearing, tell God about it in word or on paper.

We love because he first loved us. (1 John 4:19)

FOOD FOR THOUGHT AND REFLECTION

Jesus once said something like this to some would-be followers, "What kind of love is love if you only love those who love you back? Anyone with a pulse is capable of that" (Mt 5:46-47, my paraphrase). But real love has little to do with what we get in return. Real love has more to do with generously giving oneself away for the sake of another than it does with anything that weighs the scales of who gets what out of the deal. That's why God's love is so amazing, so pure. We have nothing of value that will add to God. He has everything we need. In fact, He is everything we need. And yet, we never hear God say, "What's in this for me? Give me some idea about how you plan to benefit me in this relationship and I'll consider loving you." Nothing could be further from the truth.

Truth be known, the only reason we love at all is because God first loved us (I John 4:19). We wouldn't have a clue about giving love, receiving love, or even describing what love looked like if God had not loved us first. God is love. And even in our messed up understanding and practice of what love is all about, God continues to love us and draw us to Himself out of love. "I have loved you with an everlasting love; I have drawn you with unfailing kindness," God tells us (Jeremiah 31:3).

God offers us a gift we can neither earn nor repay. In offering us His love, God offers us Himself—for God is love. The question is "How tightly will we grasp hold of the love that first took hold of us?"

RESPOND

Do you think that you would love God if He didn't love you first?

What if somehow you could love God, but He let you down—disappointed you, didn't give you what you asked for, or even walked away from your love? Do you think you'd continue to love Him as He has continued to love you?

Finish this sentence honestly and sincerely as a note or letter you could somehow mail to God—from your heart to His ears (make it as short or as long as needed or desired): "God, because you first loved ME …"

RECEIVE

Cup your hands together in front of you as if to receive a gift or to hold some water poured from a pitcher. Insert your name into the sentence as you hear these words of blessing and identity from God's heart to yours:

You are my beloved, _____, I delight in you, and with you I am well pleased.

DAY 3
A GOD WHO SINGS AND DANCES OVER YOU

It's only day three, but perhaps you're already beginning to get the feeling that God really does have a thing for you. You may live in a sea of humanity, but somehow, in a way that only God can do, He not only takes notice of you, He actually knows your name and takes interest in you. And no matter where you've been or what you have or haven't done, His opinion of you hasn't changed—He delights in you with singing and dancing.

◁▷
RE-POSITION

Take a few moments to quiet yourself. Two things we often neglect in our busyness—learning to breathe deeply and learning to be quiet. Practice doing both. As you're doing so, think about what kind of attention you would want to give Jesus if He were sitting across from you. Slow down to that extent as you give Jesus your full presence.

An early 20th century chorus suggests a great way to begin your meeting with Jesus. After reading it (or singing it if you know it), put your heart and mind into doing what it says.

> *"Turn your eyes upon Jesus, look full in his wonderful face,*
> *and the things of earth will grow strangely dim in the light of*
> *His glory and grace."*

RENEW

God's promises are true, and He always keeps them. And His promises are not just for everyone else, they also include you. That being so, the passage below will hopefully bring you great joy and encouragement.

Underline the words "is" and "will" as you read the following passage. Read the passage again and emphasize the words you underlined. Thank God at each occurrence for who He "is" and what He "will" do. Make it as personal as possible. For instance, "Thank you God that you take delight in me with gladness."

For the Lord your God is living among you. He is a mighty savior. He will take delight in you with gladness. With His love, he will calm all of your fears. He will rejoice over you with joyful songs. (Zephaniah 3:17)

FOOD FOR THOUGHT AND REFLECTION

It is easy to imagine a Prince Charming who might sing and dance over us. Children and grown-ups alike need not look far for a book or a movie spun with yarns of waltzes and fairy dust. Let us be up-front and honest, it is also easy for us to imagine that females, in general, have a far greater appreciation for song and dance fairytales. Moreover, those are nice stories, but they are not real life.

If this is truthful information, how can each of us, male and female, make any kind of sense of the concept of God rejoicing over us with joyful songs and exultation that results in dancing? Over us?

Yes, it is a true story! The God of all creation—who spun the planets and the starry hosts into space, who fashioned us from the dust of the earth, who came as a tiny infant born to become the Rescuer—looks upon His beloved children and He sings and dances over us all. Who is this King of glory who delights in us so?

It is the same One who knows the very moment your heart bore a wound because your dad didn't see you. It is the same One who counts the tears you cry because you danced your best dance or pitched your best game but your parents did not come, the One who knows how much you love children, the One who feels your loneliness, the One who whispers your name when the noise of the world is still.

God's story is no fairytale. His love is for real. It's for us all. No exceptions. Jesus is among us, and He is a mighty Savior who delights in us.

RESPOND

Make a list of several ways (5-10) you can imagine that God might delight in (sing and dance over) a newborn baby:

Now make a list of all the reasons you think that God might not want to delight in or sing and dance so much over you:

Now, cross out or rip up the list you just made describing you. The beauty of God's delight is that it isn't contingent on what you do or don't do. God simply delights in you because He loves you. In fact, God's delight in you will look an awful lot like the ways you expressed God's delight in the newborn you described. Take some time to make that first list personal and thank God for the ways He delights in you far beyond what you earn or deserve. It might go something like this, "Thank you God for smiling when you see me smile." Now, it's your turn.

RECEIVE

Hear God's words, living and true, once again from Zephaniah 3:17. Insert your own name as you do:

_____, I am with you. I am your savior. I take delight in you with joyful gladness. I will calm all your fears. Know that as you go on your way today, I'll be rejoicing over you with singing!

DAY 4
A GOD WHO SHARES HIMSELF WITH YOU

Why would a prince ever dine with a pauper? Why would a king ever share his kingdom plans with a commoner? Yet, that's exactly what God does with us. God not only gives us life — He shares His very life with us. This God who delights in us, to the point of singing and dancing over us, actually opens His heart to us so that we might know and enjoy Him.

⊲▷

RE-POSITION

If possible, change your vantage point. If it's feasible, go to a second story or higher viewing spot. If you can't get higher, maybe get lower. Perhaps you can lie on the floor. Ponder just how big God is. Look at the thousands of things around you that He's created—from a carpet thread or blade of grass to an expansive mountain range or the vast amount of iron ore that causes a skyscraper to stand tall. As you look at all the countless works of God's hand, ask as the psalmist did, "What is mankind that you are mindful of them, human beings that you care for them?" (Psalm 8:4). Give thanks to a God so big for loving you, a creation so small.

RENEW

Carefully and intentionally read through the passage below. Pause and listen. Write down anything you hear God saying (or maybe even possibly saying) to you. Next, read through the passage a second time and circle all the personal pronouns in the passage (I, you, me, my, them). What do you hear God saying about how personally connected your relationship is with Him?

I will not leave you as orphans; I will come to you. Before long, the world will not see me anymore, but you will see me. Because I live, you also will live. On that day you will realize that I am in my Father, and you are in me, and I am in you. Whoever has my commands and keeps them is the one who loves me. The one who loves me will be loved by my Father, and I too will love them and show myself to them. (John 14:18-21)

FOOD FOR THOUGHT AND REFLECTION

Generous. That's what God is. He has it all, owns it all … in fact, He made it all—everything we see and even the things we don't. It all belongs to Him. He owes no one anything, and no compelling arguments exist as to why He should have to share with us even one thing He has formed or crafted. And yet, God does share—all of it. And that's what makes Him so kind, so giving. The earth, the animals, the waters and skies—even other human beings—all shared with us to bring life, sustain life, and enjoy life.

And that would be enough. In fact, more than enough—far beyond what we remotely deserve. But God's heart is big. He does not pay us (or even re-pay us) according to what we deserve, but constantly tips the scales in our direction. He doesn't have to. Certainly no one can make Him. But that's what He does out of his deep and generous spirit of love.

And here's the kicker. Here's what should really blow our minds. The maker of "field and forest, vale and mountain, flowery meadow, flashing sea"—the One who made and rules over it all (including you and me)—not only shares what He has made, but actually shares something of infinitely greater value: Himself.

God actually shares Himself with us! And He does so in the most extravagant way in Jesus. In sending His most treasured gift, His Son, God made possible the opportunity to know the love of the Father by knowing the love of His Son. God's desire in all this? That you may begin "to be filled to the measure of all the fullness of God." Yes, God wants to share Himself with us—that's just the kind of loving and generous God He is.

RESPOND

Ask God this question, "God, why are you mindful of me?" Listen, then write down whatever you hear.

Ask God to show Himself to you in any way He desires. If His response isn't immediate, trust Him in the process. When He does speak, what will you do with what He shares or asks?

What are some things you would like to know about God? Ask God if He would show you more of Himself, in His own way, in His own timing, and in a way that will make sense to you when needed.

RECEIVE

Insert your name here as you hear God say:

Dear _____, "my thoughts are not your thoughts, neither are your ways my ways. As the heavens are higher than the earth, so are my ways higher than your ways and my thoughts than your thoughts. Still, I long to give Myself to you. And as I do, "my word that goes out from my mouth it will not return to me empty, but will accomplish what I desire and achieve [in you and in my Kingdom] the purpose for which I sent it. You, _____, will go out in joy and be led forth in peace" to the glory and honor of My name. Amen (may it be so). (Isaiah 55:8-12, adapted)

DAY 5
A GOD WHO KNOWS YOU INTIMATELY

We often are impressed when the principal of our school or the president of the company we work for somehow knows us in a more personal way. How much more should it astound us that the God of the universe, the creator of heaven and earth, the One who hung the stars and stocked the seas — knows us in intimate detail? Amazingly, it's true. God knows our name and cares for the smallest details of our life.

◁▷
RE-POSITION

Look around you. Look at everything created—large and small. Hopefully you have a view of the outside world. Focus on any one object that you see … it may be a desk, chair, or coffee cup, or perhaps a tree, flower, or bird. You choose. For just a few moments, contemplate how much there is to know about that object—how it's made, what parts it contains, how all its components work and move together, who designed and crafted the first one, what makes it unique and beautiful, and how that object makes the world or living even a little better because it exists.

Now think for a moment how God may study you in a similar manner. Genuinely thank Him for being "acquainted with all your ways," and ask Him, as the clay might request of the potter, "Will you mold me and make me according to your beautiful design, O Lord?"

RENEW

Read the following passage carefully and intentionally two or three times through. After each reading, pause. Listen to what God might be saying to you—about that passage or anything else. Allow God to set the agenda. After all, He knows you much better than you even think you know yourself.

O Lord, you have examined my heart and know everything about me.
(Psalm 139:1)

FOOD FOR THOUGHT AND REFLECTION

On the one hand, we desire so deeply to be known. On the other hand, we shy away from opportunities to be known because we fear being exposed and then being rejected. It is a delicate line we walk, trying to keep the proper balance of being known and being protected. The words of David in Psalm 139 explore so thoroughly the beauty, freedom, and safety of being fully known by our Creator.

So many times, the filter through which we see God creates a view of Him that is muted and pale; we see Him as disappointed, and even angry. In this Psalm of David, when we read that "God knows our thoughts and that we cannot escape from His Spirit," we can be tempted to think that God is "onto us." During this time of daring to grow in intimacy with God, take the opportunity to be brave and ask God to show Himself to you without the fuzzy filters.

How profound to grasp the knowledge that God's thoughts toward us are precious, that His thoughts toward us are so numerous that we cannot even count them! If we run from Him, He is already in the place we run to. In the darkness, His light cannot be snuffed. He is in front of us, behind us, and around us. He knows us, down to the way our bodies are put together.

We are His divine workmanship, His marvelous creations. He knows the complexities of our hearts, our minds, our souls, our bodies. He knows all of the beautiful things and all of the not so beautiful things, and everything in between.

RESPOND

Re-write Psalm 139:1 in your own words:

What does the truth of that verse mean for you or anyone else who reads it?

Ask God to examine your heart. Write down whatever you hear.

RECEIVE

As before, insert your name into this sentence as you hear God speak …

_____, I know you inside and out — every bone in your body. I know exactly how you were made, bit by bit. I sculpted you from nothing into something. Like an open book, I watched you grow from conception to birth. All the stages of your life were spread out before Me. I've had all the days of your life prepared for you before you even lived one day. Wherever you go, whatever you do, I am there. You mean that much to Me. (Adapted from Psalm 139, The Message)

DAY 6
A GOD WHO PURSUES YOU

Pursuing God makes sense. After all, He's God — altogether glorious, great, good, and gracious. He's worth the chase in whatever degree we can catch up with Him. What's much harder for most of us to fathom is that this God so worth pursuing actually pursues us. What do we possibly have to offer Him? Is it possible that He simply loves us that much?

◁▷
RE-POSITION

Take some deep breaths and exhale any tiring thoughts or struggles you've been carrying in all your pursuits of life and God today (the good, the bad, and the ugly). Sometimes when we simply slow down enough from all our running and flailing about, we see that God has been just steps behind us waiting for us to stop long enough for Him to join us.

Acknowledge to God that He is with you. Whether or not you "feel" Him near, He is present with you as promised. Thank Him for loving you and pursuing you beyond how you may feel about your love and life on any given day.

RENEW

Imagination is a wonderful gift. It's unfortunate that so many think that they have to somehow put it away when they become an adult. Resist that urge. With childlike wonder and faith, allow yourself to get lost in the story that Jesus tells below. First, imagine you are a lost sheep. What does that feel like? What's going on around you in strange and unfamiliar places? What do you fear? What do you hope for? Second, put yourself in the role of the shepherd. What are you thinking, feeling, longing for? Third, imagine God as the shepherd and you as the sheep. What do you hope for from the shepherd? What do you want to say or do when found?

Suppose one of you has a hundred sheep and loses one of them. Doesn't he leave the ninety-nine in the open country and go after the lost sheep until he finds it? (Luke 15:4)

FOOD FOR THOUGHT AND REFLECTION

Very few of us have to be reminded that "all we, like sheep, have gone astray" (Isaiah 53:6). Our lives demonstrate that truth most every day. What we may need to be reminded of is a God who loves lost, messed up, foolish, and pit-finding sheep. So much does God love His sheep that He pursues them, goes looking for them—even when they're lost due to their own bone-headed choices.

God loves to go after lost things—lost sheep, lost coins, and lost sons and daughters. He's the best kind of shepherd that way. He's the kind of shepherd that puts His own life at risk for the sheep that He loves—simply because they are of value and worth to Him. King David, who did a little shepherding himself, knew intimately about the Good Shepherd who chases after those whom He loves. David knew that whether he lived his life in the heavens or made his bed in hell (Psalm 139), God was present and pursuing.

God doesn't pursue us to bludgeon us. He pursues us because He thinks that much of us. He does so, not based on our performance or anything we can offer Him, but simply out of His deep love for us. He doesn't want us to miss out on the life He intended for us when He knit us together in our mother's womb.

Imagine, God goes after the likes of you and me. Is there any greater thought to know that God thinks we're worth pursuing?

RESPOND

Use your imagination once again. You're on a stranded island. What kind of "message in a bottle" do you want to write to God that might help Him find and rescue you?

Some people fear being found by God—Adam and Eve did. Sometimes we aren't ready for God to find us in the mess we've made or are in. But God isn't as interested in your "good state" or "good housekeeping" nearly as much as He is interested in you. Jesus is knocking at your door. Are you going to answer it? What are you going to say to Him if you do open the door?

RECEIVE

Imagine you're out looking for God when all the while He's been looking for you. Hear deep within you the same encouragement and hope the people of Israel did in their desert place:

> "Israel, out looking for a place to rest, met God out looking for them." God told them, "I've never quit loving you and never will. Expect love, love, and more love." (Jeremiah 31:2-3, The Message).

Now hear it from God's mouth to your ears:

> _____, while you've been looking for a place to rest, I've been out searching for you! I've never quit loving you and never will. Expect love, love, and more love.

DAY 7
A GOD WHO CALLS YOU BACK HOME

What kind of love leaves the light on for you? God's love. No matter where you've gone, how long ago you left, or on what terms you departed, God has always said, "There's a place at home for you."

◁▷
RE-POSITION

As you re-position your heart, mind, and soul toward God today, allow Scripture to lead you. After praying and asking God to meet you on His terms and in His timing, read the following passage over with great sincerity and intentionality. Express to God your desire for the truth of this passage to be so.

Surely goodness and mercy shall follow me all the days of my life, and I shall dwell in the house of the Lord forever. (Psalm 23:6)

✚
RENEW

The following passage is one of the most well-told and well-liked stories in all of Scripture. It's the story of a loving Father and his two lost sons—one who leaves home and the other who stays. In both cases, the story's focus is on the gracious and extravagant love of the Father who welcomes his lost sons home. We relate so powerfully to the story because it's each one of our stories too. As you read, picture the outstretched arms of your heavenly Father who, before you can get a single fumbling excuse from your lips says, "Welcome home!"

But while he was still far off, his father saw him and was filled with compassion; he ran and put his arms around him and kissed him. (Luke 15:20)

FOOD FOR THOUGHT AND REFLECTION

While he was far off ... while he had not yet confessed. While he was still an undignified and dirty degenerate. While he had not one inherited penny to return. While he had not written, called, or sent word since his leaving. While the tarnish on the family name was still fresh. While the old drama was still new. While the wounds inflicted on his father's heart were still open ... that's when his father, "filled with compassion," ran to him. He did not meander, saunter, strut, lumber, stomp, shuffle, walk, or even jog. He ran. He couldn't get to his son fast enough to throw his arms around him, restore him to peace, and welcome him back home. All this, not for the father's sake, but for the son's. And we say, what a father.

What a Father indeed. God wants us home. While He loves us enough to let us foolishly leave, He stands on the porch longing for our return. He lovingly leaves the light on for us.

Psalm 116 tells us all in one breath that while God is righteous, He is equally gracious and full of compassion, and that He protects and saves those who are brought low (Ps 116:5-6). Such knowledge urges the psalm-writer toward only one reasonable response: "Return to your rest, my soul, for the Lord has been good to you" (v. 7).

A loving Father who wants His children home. That may not be your family history, but it is God's. Whether near or far from God, know that you have a Father who constantly scans the horizon for the first sign of you—to welcome you home.

RESPOND

Re-write Luke 15:20, only this time, make it personal. "While I was still off, my Father …" After finishing the verse, tell God what that means to you … what He means to you.

Is there anything keeping you from going home or being at home with God? If so, talk to Him about it. Like the younger son in the story in Luke 15, is there anything for which you need to say, "Father, please forgive me"?

RECEIVE

_____, if you make yourself at home with me and my words are at home in you, you can be sure that whatever you ask, today and every day, will be listened to and acted upon. (John 15:7, The Message)

WEEK 2
Our Love Story

"We were made for God alone."
O that we would have believed and trusted that.
But we didn't, and we often still don't.
Although made to walk with God, it seemed wiser to us at some
point to go it alone. And what a mess we made, and continue to
make, of things.
Still, our messy story remains a part of God's much larger
story of love that calls us to grasp hold of the life He always
intended for us to share with Him.

DAY 8
A STORY WITH PURPOSE

On the day you were born, God did not suddenly scratch His head and exclaim, "Where did you come from?" You may be one among the billions who move about this earth — still, God knows you by name and has your good and His glory in mind when He thinks of you. Your story is not accidental. Quite the contrary — God knows the plans He has for you. You were made with purpose, on purpose, to know and glorify God.

RE-POSITION

When we meet up with friends, rarely do we jump into deep or heavy conversation upon arrival. We often begin with some moments of "catch-up." Spend some moments catching up with God. Tell Him how your day has gone so far, what you've been up to lately, or about a book you're reading, a team you're following, a hobby you're enjoying, etc. Be sure to take some time to ask God how things are going with Him.

RENEW

This is a good place to insert your name in a Scripture passage. After all, as mind-blowing as it may seem, God actually had you in mind along with the Israelite people He was addressing through His prophet Jeremiah. After the first "you" in the sentence, insert your name. Listen for God's voice as you read. Can you hear Him say, "I, the King of kings and Lord of lords, know the plans I have for you, _____"?

"For I know the plans I have for you", declares the Lord, "plans to prosper you and not to harm you, plans to give you hope and a future." (Jeremiah 29:11)

FOOD FOR THOUGHT AND REFLECTION

When it comes to your life, do you ever feel like a garage door handle on a house equipped with an automatic door opener? It looks good and is nice enough to have around, but you wonder if it's really all that important or necessary.

As human beings, we often ask questions about whether or not our lives have purpose. We do so because something deep within us instinctively knows that we were created "on purpose, with purpose." A whisper within speaks to us that we were created in love, to be loved, and to share love. Jesus stated our intended purpose quite clearly: "to have life, and have it to the fullest extent" in a deep and abiding love relationship with God (John 10:10).

Unfortunately, the clear voice of purpose, goodness, and life spoken to us by God often gets muddled and muted by another voice—the voice of the enemy—who whispers doubt, deceit, and ultimately, destruction. Our confusion begins when we entertain the thought, as Adam and Eve did, "Did God really say that?" Deceived, many spend a lifetime believing that being created "very good" for God alone isn't good enough. So they go it alone—trying to write their own story that will somehow bring purpose and meaning to life.

God's purposes for you, and in you, matter. He's never wavered in His plans for you—plans that are ultimately good and eternally meaningful (Jeremiah 29:11). You may feel like you are one among millions of people in this world, but to God, you are one in a million. In fact, God marvels at you. You may not think so, but it's true. Your story is a "very good" one that has its lines in a much larger novel that God is penning. The question is, will you trust Him to write or will you hold the pen when the plot gets shaky?

RESPOND

If you have a calendar or planner handy, pull it out (paper, phone, computer, etc.). Look at all the plans—plans you have made for you and that others have made for you. Consider the busyness that fills your life. Does all your planning matter? Is it going anywhere?

Now take some time to consider God's plans for you. Where does He fit in your calendar? Where do you fit in His? Take time to flip some pages or scroll down through various days, weeks, or months. Ask God if there are any time slots that need to be filled with His name. It could be for time alone with Him, something He wants you to do or experience, or simply created space that He'll fill in later as you need to know. If you hear God speak (or even think He might be speaking), write it down or fill in days and dates with whatever you hear.

RECEIVE

Return to your day with these truths in hand:

But the plans of the Lord stand firm forever, the purposes of his heart through all generations. (Psalm 33:11)

The Lord knows all human plans; he knows that they are futile. (Psalm 94:11)

Commit to the Lord whatever you do, and he will establish your plans. (Proverbs 16:3)

A STORY WITH A PAST, PRESENT, AND FUTURE

God is writing a beautiful narrative, and good news — you're in it! The entrance and insertion of your life in the plans and purposes of God is right on cue. While the present script you hold in your hands may not completely make sense to you, be assured that God is weaving your past and present into a never-ending story well worth the read.

RE-POSITION

Begin your time with God today by looking back. Take some time to remember and re-count the ways that God has faithfully met you in the past. Maybe it's a healthy body, maybe a loving family, maybe a time when He "saw you through." Begin to turn your heart and thoughts to Him by thinking and thanking. "Give thanks to the Lord," Psalm 136 tells us, "for he is good, and his steadfast love endures forever."

If you have time to read all of Psalm 136, you may find other ways to recount God's goodness and give thanks. If not, breathe easy, God is here to meet you where you are.

RENEW

Short passages in the Bible, in particular, are wonderful to meditate upon. Take some time to be still. Read the following verse slowly and carefully. If you're in a place that will permit it, read the verse out loud. Pause. Allow God's living words to settle and soak in for a few moments. Read the passage again one or two more times in the same way you did the first time. Give God space and time to say whatever He wants as you sit with this verse. Engage with God in conversation—ask questions, tell God what you hear or even think you hear. The goal is an "I with you, you with me" encounter.

There is a time for everything, and a season for every activity under the heavens. (Ecclesiastes 3:1)

FOOD FOR THOUGHT AND REFLECTION

Have you ever wondered why you were born in this present era of time and not another? Some folks are sure that they would have been better suited in the roaring 20's, the Victorian Age, the Iron Age, the 1950's, the Wild West, etc. Maybe you have an era wish of your own. A young lady named Esther wondered if perhaps her life was on the right stage. "Why here, why now?" she pondered. "For such a time as this," came the reply from her Uncle Mordecai (Esther 4:14). God had plans for Esther in the larger plans He was up to. Her life was perfectly positioned in time and space.

Even Jesus was born "in the fullness of time," Galatians 4:4 tells us. His arrival in history 2,000 plus years ago was no accident. God strategically placed Him in time and space as a part of a much larger plan. Jesus' life came in the midst of an orchestrated past and future. His present story was right on time. And so is yours.

You may not know the bigger picture of why God has you here and now in history. That's okay, you weren't meant to have it all figured out. But you were meant to trust God in the process.

You can't re-write your past. You can't prescribe the future. But you can draw near to God who can do both of those things. As you listen for and to His voice and follow Him in faith, He will pen the script for your life that fits perfectly into His larger story. In so doing, you will come to know that there has been no mistake—you are here "for such a time as this."

RESPOND

Make a list of 5-6 ways your life might have been different if you lived in another day and time (like the early 1900's when electricity, cars, and phones of any kind were rare).

Why do you think God may have you living and breathing "here and now" in this day and age? Ask Him. Write down whatever is on your heart or runs through your mind.

RECEIVE

_____, I know the plans I have for you — plans to prosper you and not to harm you, plans to give you hope and a future. Please hear that, it's true. Call on Me, and come and pray to Me, and I will listen to you. When you seek Me with all your heart, please know, you will find Me ... I'm here to be found. (Jeremiah 29:11-13, paraphrased)

DAY 10
A STORY WITH BAGGAGE

If you've ever traveled through the airport or a bus station without luggage, you most likely know how much easier and freeing the traveling experience is without it. Unfortunately, when it comes to life and love, none of us journey without dragging some kind of cumbersome baggage along that ends up weighing us down and slowing us up. But good news once again— God always welcomes us when we come to Him, baggage and all. In fact, if we'll trust Him, He'll carry our bags all the way home and sort out all the unnecessary "stuff" along the way.

RE-POSITION

One of the best ways to present ourselves fully to God in any moment is through humility. Genuine humility is not found by thinking too little of ourselves, but by thinking more highly and more often of others. In today's encounter, humility is about thinking about who God is (high and lifted up, holy, altogether glorious, great, good, gracious, etc.) and who we are in comparison to such a holy God.

If possible, pray on your knees or even lay face down on the floor before God. If that's not possible, do your best to bow submissively in your heart as you discover what the prophet Isaiah did when he encountered God in His holiness:

"Woe to me!" I cried. "I am ruined! For I am a person of unclean lips, and I live among a people of unclean lips, and my eyes have seen the King, the Lord Almighty." (Isaiah 6:5)

RENEW

Read the passage below purposefully one time through. Sit quietly with the passage for a moment. Write down any thoughts, comments, or questions that come to you as you listen.

Read the passage again, but this time substitute the word "I" for the words "men and women" and "they." After a second reading, let God and His words sit with you a bit. Express in word or writing anything you might want or need to share with God.

This is the crisis we're in: God-light streamed into the world, but men and women everywhere ran for the darkness. They went for the darkness because they were not really interested in pleasing God. Everyone who makes a practice of doing evil, addicted to denial and illusion, hates God-light and won't come near it, fearing a painful exposure. But anyone working and living in truth and reality welcomes God-light so the work can be seen for the God-work it is. (John 3:19-21 The Message)

FOOD FOR THOUGHT AND REFLECTION

Dear God, how many times must I return to You and really listen to Your words over me that my junk is overhauled, that I'm forgiven and free, that my baggage does not define me? I'm so weary of this pattern. And yet, I have a choice right now in this moment. Pick up the bags and let them weigh me down on the journey, let them be my identifiers. Or run straight to the safety of Your heart until I remember who I am.

The truth is that we all have a past. In this world there's a whole lot of trouble, and we are bound to feel it and know it firsthand. The extent of the pains we bear does vary, and for some, the pieces of our past are easier to release. However, the pains we bear are ours. Each heart knows its own wounds (Proverbs 14:10), and the wounds ache and bleed. Whether our history is pocked with harms given to us or harms we have given to another, many of us have learned to hide in our shame, naked and afraid.

Can we trust that God, who formed us in the secrecy of the womb, can handle our nakedness and our fear, our shame, and our deep hurt? If we heard the voice of God calling—not calling to our damage for disappointment's sake or condemnation's sake—but calling to us as His beloved for whom He desperately longs, could we release the grip on our baggage long enough to be able to run into His love and healing?

The past did indeed happen. We cannot undo it. But it need not be the definitive marker of the days to come.

RESPOND

Adam said to God in the Garden, "I heard you … but I was afraid because I was naked; so I hid" (Genesis 3:10). Do you trust God to love you if you're honest with Him about all the baggage you carry? God calls us to come closer to Him … it is we who run and hide out of guilt and shame. Make a list of some of the entanglements of guilt or shame that have slowed you down and held you back with God and others:

Is there anything you need to confess to God that's been keeping you far from Him? Take whatever time is needed to confess (agree with God) whatever sin or baggage is weighing you down and keeping you back. Ask God to forgive you for carrying things that don't belong on this journey or in your relationship with Him.

RECEIVE

Cup your hands to receive this gift. If it's a freeing posture for you, extend your arms above your head the way a toddler would request a parent or loved one to pick them up and hold them:

_____, if you claim that you're free of sin, you're only fooling yourself. A claim like that is errant nonsense. On the other hand, when you admit your sins — make a clean breast of them — I won't let us down; I'll be true to myself. I'll forgive your sins and purge you of all wrongdoing. (1 John 1:8-9, The Message)

When I make you free, you are truly free. Be free!

DAY 11
A STORY WITH BARRIERS

Have you ever been delayed or re-routed by a detour when you're trying to get somewhere that you really want to go? If you're like most, the experience becomes frustrating, anxiety producing, and sometimes makes you want to turn around and just go back home. Our journey with God is full of roadblocks, detours, and barriers. While Satan has destructive ideas of His own, God wants to actually use such obstacles to draw you closer to Him.

RE-POSITION

As you begin today, share with God any challenges or distractions that you may be experiencing as you meet (tired, an undone "to do" list, feeling distant from Him or others, feeling lazy or bored, etc.). Be really honest with God—He really does know what it's like to be human.

As you come to each obstacle, place it into God's hands—ask Him to set aside or remove altogether whatever would keep you from spending quality time with Him today.

If today is a particularly "good" day where such obstacles don't seem to exist, give thanks to God and ask Him to help you remember this approach on another needed day.

✛

RENEW

Ask God to open the eyes of your heart and mind as you read the passage below. Ask the Lord, "What do you want me to see here? What do you want me to know or learn?"

If you have time, go back and read about all the inductees in the "Hall of Faith" in Hebrews 11 in order to help you discover what the "therefore" in Hebrews 12:1 is "there for."

Therefore, since we are surrounded by such a great cloud of witnesses, let us throw off everything that hinders and the sin that so easily entangles. And let us run with perseverance the race marked out for us, fixing our eyes on Jesus, the pioneer and perfecter of faith. For the joy set before him he endured the cross, scorning its shame, and sat down at the right hand of the throne of God. (Hebrews 12:1-2)

FOOD FOR THOUGHT AND REFLECTION

There are a lot of things that come between God and us. A forever nagging "you don't really want what He wants" rings in the caverns of our daily decisions. Yes, sometimes it is our past. But there's plenty of "dangers, toils, and snares" right in the present. Be well assured, "Your enemy the devil prowls around like a roaring lion looking for someone to devour" (I Peter 5:8).

Barriers seek to stop us, detour us, or have us turn back altogether. The enemy would love nothing more than to keep you from God's love. He knows he can't stop you when you take refuge in God and "taste and see that the Lord is good" (Psalm 34:8). His hope is to distract with a thousand lesser things. To turn your attention toward things right in front of you that you can see and seek to convince you that the God you can't see is an unobtainable fantasy. Faulty filters, distortions, untruths.

But here's some doubly good news. First, there's nothing that can separate you from God's love. No matter how big the barrier or how far we've strayed in detours and delays, there's no force or thing that can rip us away from a deepening love relationship with God (Romans 8:38-39). Second, the roadblocks employed by the enemy can actually make us more God dependent and drive us deeper and farther into the arms of God's love if we'll pay attention.

We've all made a mess of things with our lives. We've all fallen short and have taken the bait to follow a thousand other lovers that will never satisfy. While that's our story, God has a better one with a better plot and ending. Our job is to "seek God with our whole heart" (Jeremiah 29:13). When we do, no matter the barrier or the distance of the detour ... God helps us find our way.

RESPOND

Take some time to think about all the challenges and obstacles in Jesus' life—had to be hidden as a baby, tempted by Satan in the wilderness, all the people who didn't understand Him, the religious leaders constantly undermining Him, often "alone" in His ministry and mission, having to suffer and die though completely innocent, etc.

Talk to Jesus about the challenges He faced. Share with Jesus about the barriers that have kept, or are keeping you, from knowing Him and serving Him in a deeper way.

RECEIVE

_____, nothing can separate you from my love. Death can't. Life can't. Neither can angels nor demons, neither the present nor the future, nor any powers, neither height nor depth, nor anything else in all creation. No person, no thing, no sin, no circumstance, no doubt, will ever be able to separate you from my love. (Romans 8:38-39)

DAY 12
A STORY WITH A PROMISED HAPPY ENDING

Here's the loveliness of our story. Whether our life story has been a fantasy, a comedy, or a tragedy, God continues to write our story with a beautiful ending. Our lifetime may be filled with nights of crying our eyes out, but as we abide in Christ, nights of sorrow give way to days of joy and laughter.

RE-POSITION

Take some time to think about your favorite movie, book, comic book series, or television show. Why is it your favorite? Are there any connections between you and any of the characters or plot line? What do you hope happens as the story ends?

Ask God to make any needed connections as you meet with Him today. Ask Him to use anything and everything around you to help you connect your real life to His real love.

RENEW

The apostle John was a "revelator." Beyond being a really cool sounding super hero name, it simply means that John listened for God and wrote down whatever he saw. Why don't you do the same? Spend some time listening to God after you read this passage, and then write down or draw whatever you hear or see.

And I heard a loud voice from the throne saying, "Look! God's dwelling place is now among the people, and he will dwell with them. They will be his people, and God himself will be with them and be their God. He will wipe every tear from their eyes. There will be no more death or mourning or crying or pain, for the old order of things has passed away." (Revelation 21:3-5)

FOOD FOR THOUGHT AND REFLECTION

"Life is pain," said Prince Humperdink in the 1987 movie classic, The Princess Bride. "Anyone who tells you differently is selling you something." While the prince and the movie are fictitious, the statement is much closer to truth than reality. Life is rife with pain, setbacks, drawbacks, and challenges. That's why so many seek to escape, medicate, and mask the hard realities of life. We constantly look for an oasis, a hiding place, a happy place.

Perhaps you remember or have seen re-runs of another 1980's classic—the award-winning sit-com, Cheers. The theme song affirmed, "We want to go to a place where everybody knows our name," suggesting that in a world of difficulty, we want to go to a place where we can find some relief from the hard realities of life.

Scripture, however, doesn't paint a picture of earthly prosperity, where, if we just say "yes" to God, then all will be well and good, everyone will like us, no one will unduly harm us, and the cupboards will always be full in the "big rock candy mountain" house of our choosing. The promise of Jesus is quite the contrary. "In this life you will have trouble" He promises in John 16:33. Like a race to be run and a battle to be won, our lives with or without God come with hardship and challenge. The difference a life of intimate fellowship with God makes is how we run the race, fight the battle, and what awaits us when our earthly story comes to a close.

Jesus adds to the life-is-trouble passage above, "But take heart ... I have overcome the world." Not only does Jesus provide what is needed to overcome the hard people and places of this life, He also promises us that as we walk with Him, the best is (by far) yet to come.

RESPOND

Think for a moment how your life might be temporarily better if you chose to go it alone without Jesus. Consider also some of the ways that life with Jesus has actually brought on some trouble of its own. Now answer the following questions as honestly as possible:

Why am I in relationship with Jesus and what am I after?

What do I/did I expect that a life journeying closely with Jesus would look like?

Is whatever pain I face now worth the gain then?

RECEIVE

The apostle John heard a loud voice from heaven speaking to him. May you also hear God as He says to you …

_____, here is what you have to look forward to as you continue to abide in me. I will dwell with you. I will be with you and be your God. No matter what you faced in your earthly life, I will wipe every tear from your eyes. Get this — in heaven, there will be no more death or mourning or crying or pain, for the old order of things has passed away. I am making everything, including you, new! (Revelation 21:3-5, adapted)

DAY 13
A STORY WITH A HUNGER TO KNOW AND BE KNOWN

We want to know. We want to be known. All of our questioning, pondering, speaking, relating, and doing points to those two facts. And at the heart of it all is the deepest desire to know and be known by God.

RE-POSITION

Changing our physical posture sometimes helps us to re-position our spiritual posture. Try praying in a posture of humility. If you are able, get on your knees with your head bowed in submission before God. If that posture is physically limiting, bow your head and body as much as you are able. The idea is to present yourself in a way that acknowledges God's bigness and your smallness.

Ask God if He would make more of Himself known to you today. Ask Him to show you more of the real you—the good, bad, and ugly. Commit to be as honest as you know how to be in the process.

RENEW

Knowing and being known is risky business. The risk of being known opens wider the possibility to be exposed, misunderstood, or rejected. That's why most of us keep our heart and thoughts guarded. Before you read the passage below, clench your fist tightly. Then, slowly open your hand as a gesture of trust to receive whatever God wants to show you as you study, read, and pray.

You have searched me, Lord, and you know me. (Psalm 139:1)

FOOD FOR THOUGHT AND REFLECTION

The garden. When it was just the created originals—Adam and his beloved Eve—and their Creator. No hiding. Fully known. Fully knowing. Adam and Eve with one another and the Trinity with them. All wrapped, intertwined. Mysteriously and freely, no hunger unmet, no thirst un-satiated, no need left alone to beg.

It is difficult, on a good day, to imagine such a paradise. Some may even question its reality. If we look around, it seems the existence of this very real place, this very true space in time is actually proved so.

What is the flooded plane of writers, painters, musicians, architects, chemists, teachers, missionaries, public servants, janitors, poets, builders? Is it not the scores of Adam's and Eve's who long to bring a wholeness and rightness to the world's story? Descendants of our first parents, all of us, just aching to return to the very thing for which we were created? Is it not some of the deepest desires expressed—through my gifts, through your gifts—"Please know me! Please may I know you?"

The shattered versions of these desires played out in our world through pornography, substance abuse, misaligned finances, broken marriages, damaged relationships, molestations, unhealed and bleeding soul wounds—is it possible that these, too, are fueled by the same longing to know and be known? The enemy has made a terrible-awful, twisted mess of a God-given, God-inspired vision and hope that we were created to know and be known.

And we must fall somewhere in between the beauty of the longing and the mess of the longing. Do we not? Our stories all tell of both sides. Can we dare to allow our hearts to enter into the very real core of the story with God and His Body that we were created and designed with this longing in our hearts? Perhaps we can return to the beginning and allow the Lord to know us and begin to really know Him.

RESPOND

Take some time to confess to God any hidden closets, messy rooms, locked up dreams or desires that you aren't quite sure you want Him to know about. Ironically, He already knows. Confessing to God is more about agreeing with Him about what He's already aware of. Your confession will better align you with the good plans God already has for you.

Equally, share with God things in you that perhaps you feel like He doesn't know. While we can have a head knowledge that God knows all things (that He's omniscient), in our heart we may feel God is unaware, unmoved, or uninterested in who we are and what we're experiencing. Talk to God about that as well.

Ask God to share something of Himself with you. Go for a walk, sit quietly, or whatever might put you in a position to listen well. Don't underestimate the means and method God might speak and make Himself known.

RECEIVE

Receive these promises of God as you go:

But whoever loves God is known by God. (1 Corinthians 8:3)

Then Jesus declared, "I am the bread of life. Whoever comes to me will never go hungry, and whoever believes in me will never be thirsty. (John 6:35)

Blessed are those who hunger and thirst for righteousness, for they will be filled. (Matthew 5:6)

DAY 14
A STORY WITH LONGINGS AND DESIRES

Is it possible that what gets you jazzed up, energizes you, and keeps your heart, mind, body, and soul engaged for endless hours just might be an avenue God uniquely designed to connect you more intimately to His heart and plan? If you think those longings and desires don't seem overly "godly", God probably disagrees. While some hearts get misdirected, the desire to know and please God reigns deep within our human design, and God connects with those desires in ways that are as unique as our fingerprints.

RE-POSITION

Believe or not, God likes having fun and playing games. Here's one called, "Top Three." Give God your top three in the following categories:

- Top three favorite foods to eat.

- Top three places in the world you'd like to visit.

- Top three activities you like to do for fun.

Listen for a bit. See if God comments on any of your answers.

RENEW

The context of any quote is important—whether on the internet, in a book, during a conversation, or in this case, in the midst of a Scripture passage. As you read the passage below, keep in mind that Ephesians 5 begins with "walk in the way of love, just as Christ loved us and gave himself up for us" (Ephesians 5:1).

Find out what pleases the Lord. (Ephesians 5:10)

FOOD FOR THOUGHT AND REFLECTION

Christian culture dictates that desires and longings aren't always to be trusted, that some of them are bad, or selfish, or shameful, or wrong.

On the other hand, if we listen to popular culture in America and many locations across the globe, we are told that our desires are the driving force of our days and our nights. "Listen to your heart," we hear.

So, what's right? How do we make sense of any of these things if it's an either/or proposition? It can be a complicated matter.

We do have dreams and longings, hopes and desires. We do. To deny that we really want children, now or someday, to act as if we don't want to succeed in our current projects or in our marriages or in other family relationships, to pretend that we don't long for physical, spiritual, and emotional intimacy is to somehow look at ourselves in a mirror and protest the reality of the fact that we were formed as human beings.

How do we begin to make sense of the story we are in that surely contains longings and desires? How do we un-complicate the matter at least a little bit?

Find out what pleases the Lord. (Eph 5:10)

Too simplistic? Maybe. But we can begin there.

> *"Does this longing please you, Lord? Can you help me sort it out?"*

> *"Does this dream please you, Father? Does it bring glory to You? What are the next steps?"*

> *"God, take away anything that is not pleasing to you."*

By beginning here, we acknowledge that what we desire and long for more than anything is to have our hearts and souls shaped ever more and more to resemble Jesus. He was, after all, every bit as human as we are, full of desires and longings. Might we trust Him with ours?

RESPOND

Time for another "Top Three." Tell God the top three things you are most passionate about in life. Ask Him to help you to see the connection of how those desires were created in you to ultimately please Him. Take time to thank God for making your desires as uniquely as you were made.

If you don't feel passionate about anything today, let God know that too. Ask Him to help you to recognize what you desire and to see its value in His timing and plan.

RECEIVE

Receive this promise from God:

Where the Spirit of the Lord is, there is freedom.
(2 Corinthians 3:17)

May you know the freedom of a Spirit-led life that longs to please God in so many creative ways!

WEEK 3
Surrendering to Love

Falling in love with God requires a willingness
to fall to your knees.
It means taking a back seat, a second place,
as you daily say, "You first, Lord" and
"What is it, Lord, that's pleasing to you?"
It's a clear understanding that
God is worth surrendering to;
knowing that in order to gain His life,
you must first relinquish control of your own.
In the words of the missionary, Jim Elliot,
"He is no fool who gives what he cannot keep
to gain that which he cannot lose."

DAY 15
A HEART THAT ACKNOWLEDGES WHO'S IN CHARGE

"I'd rather fight you for something I don't really want, then to take what you give that I need", wrote the late songwriter, Rich Mullins. Until we settle the matter of who's really calling the shots in our lives, we will never quit trying to make God a subject in a Kingdom of our own making. However, when we acknowledge Him as sovereign Lord of all things, seen and unseen, we begin to know the truest depths of His love.

◁▷

RE-POSITION

In Psalm 46:10, God says, "Be still, and know that I am God; I will be exalted among the nations, I will be exalted in the earth." The Hebrew meaning of "be still" is far from a quiet meditation. It really means, "Shut your mouth, quit arguing with me, and concede that I am God and you are not!" It's a call to submit to God, who is trustworthy and in control.

If possible, go for a walk, run, jog, stroll, or drive. If none of those activities are possible, do the best you can in your current setting. Look around you as you move. Do your best to keep your mind from wandering a thousand different directions. Focus on these few thoughts as you see new objects come into view, "Who made that? Who controls that? Where does its beauty or purpose come from? Who's in charge of that?" Ask God to help you see Him and His world in proper perspective.

RENEW

Sometimes we gain better perspective by placing ourselves in another's shoes. For a few moments, imagine what it must be like to be God. What perspective do you gain as you speak these words to your people through your prophet Isaiah?

"With whom will you compare me or count me equal? To whom will you liken me that we may be compared?"

"Remember this, keep it in mind, take it to heart, you rebels. Remember the former things, those of long ago; I am God, and there is no other; I am God, and there is none like me. I make known the end from the beginning, from ancient times, what is still to come. I say, 'My purpose will stand, and I will do all that I please.'" (Isaiah 46:5, 8-10)

FOOD FOR THOUGHT AND REFLECTION

It's very easy to forget that God is on His throne. The world spins at the same rate it always has, yet sometimes it seems that someone surely must have pushed the lever forward to accelerate the speed. The wind blows and scatters our schedules, relationships get lost in the muddle, and we want to scream, "Somebody stop this ride! I need to breathe for a minute."

Sigh.

Our hearts battle for the lever of control. When we get pinned to the wall from the force of centrifugal motion, we clamor and scramble for something to grip. Often our hearts weary quickly, and we lash out in other ways just to keep a grip on anything. If we could quiet our hearts for just a short time, we might hear the whisper of God's voice calling out to us that He has a better idea, a better word for our frazzled hearts.

Be still. And know that I am God. There is none like Me. Your collection of controls are dry and petrified wood, idols that do not serve you. Stop serving them. Be still. I am right here.

Deep breath. Sigh again. Release the white-knuckled hold on the lever. God is for you. He is for your heart. And He's not surprised by the spinning of the tilted planet, nor is He surprised by the ways we feel fear, suffer from anxiety and worry, ache with hopes.

If this is true—if God is who He says He is—we can let our hearts rest in His love. We can trust Him to direct us toward His desired ends. We can let Him have it all.

RESPOND

Continue to look around you and begin acknowledging God's lordship over what you see. For instance, "Lord, I acknowledge that you are lord over that tree" or "God, I recognize that you are in charge of that building and all that is in it." Your list can be endless as you look around.

Next, get a little more personal. Agree with God about all the things that He's in charge of in you. For instance, "God, I acknowledge that you are Lord of my finances" or "Lord, my future is under your control," etc.

Be honest with God about some things you may have a difficult time relinquishing. As best as you know how, hand the hard things over to God. Thank God for being trustworthy as the loving Lord over all you have and are.

RECEIVE

Sovereign rulers have the ability to grant blessing on those who inhabit their kingdom. Hear God's sovereign blessing on you as you insert your name below:

_____, I am your refuge and strength, an ever-present help in trouble. Therefore, do not fear — even if the earth gives way and the mountains fall into the heart of the sea ... I am the Lord Almighty, I'm in charge of all people and things ... and I am with you! (Psalm 46:1-2, 11, paraphrased)

DAY 16
A HEART OF SURRENDER

Love is never something to be conquered. In a world where so many fight to be first, to get ahead, and to lay hold of what they readily desire, love says "lay down your rights, lay open your heart, and allow love to conquer you." If you really want to gain life, or love, you better be ready to surrender your own.

RE-POSITION

Don't forget to breathe in this process of meeting with God. It's easy to overlook the profundity of simply breathing in rhythm with the God who gave you breath. Remember to slow down and give God your full attention. When you are ready, simply tell God, "Lord, I am here and ready."

RENEW

Take a few moments to answer the following questions:

What is the greatest tangible sacrifice you could offer God in your life right now?

What might cause you to struggle or grieve if God asked you to surrender it?

What would represent in its giving how serious you are about God being more important than that thing?

When you've come up with a thoughtful and thorough answer, read the verses below:

You do not desire a sacrifice, or I would offer one. You do not want a burnt offering. The sacrifice you desire is a broken spirit. You will not reject a broken and repentant heart, O God. (Psalm 51:16-17 New Living Translation)

FOOD FOR THOUGHT AND REFLECTION

God loves people who give up. Not quitters, but relinquishers—those who lay down their life, their way and their agenda, and yield to God's better design. God loves those who give up on the idea that they are somehow in the same ballpark with Him when it comes to being strong enough, smart enough, good enough, and wise enough to live as one was created to do. The truth is, left to ourselves, we self-destruct, implode. Like sitting in the captain's seat of a rocket ship we weren't meant to pilot, we might be able to hold it together for awhile, but sooner or later the spacecraft spins out of control and we find ourselves way off course and in grave danger. Lost in time and space, we wonder what went wrong, how we managed to get so off course, and why God seems so suddenly distant.

But there's another way. A more life-giving way. It begins with shedding the lies that we've been bombarded. The lies that somehow we know better how to command our lives than God does. It begins with what Jesus called being "poor in spirit" (Matthew 5:3) and what the psalm writer, David, called having a "broken and contrite heart" (Psalm 51:17). It is acknowledging that God is the better captain of our soul, that we don't have it all put together, that our control of the cockpit has made a mess of things, and that we're more than ready to stop talking and start listening to His better plan.

This is beyond just saying "yes" to Jesus one time. This is a day by day, moment by moment, relinquishing of our lives to God. Jesus said it this way, "Whoever wants to be my disciple must deny themselves and take up their cross and follow me" (Matthew 16:24), or as The Message translation says it, "Anyone who intends to come with me has to let me lead. You're not in the driver's seat; I am."

Intimacy with God deepens when our control of things ends. May our prayer continually be, "Lord, please take the wheel."

RESPOND

What needs to go? Are there things that you are clinching with your fist that you are fearful to give to God? Be very honest with God about the things you don't want to hand over to Him. Is it comfort? Control? Fear of what someone else will think? Fear of provision or other unknowns? Whatever it is, it isn't worth holding onto compared to what God has for you. This is where your trust and love for God is on the line. It's going to require a step of faith—trusting Him with things you cannot see or fully understand.

As honestly as you know how, lay whatever God is speaking to you about upon the altar of sacrifice. Tell God, "I gladly lay this down for love of you." Such a statement is easy to say, but much harder to really mean. It won't matter unless you mean it with all your heart. Sometimes literally or mentally "laying things on the table" helps. Put everything you can think of on the table. Allow God to decide in His timing what He takes from the table and what He tells you to place back in your hands.

Ask God to help you trust Him with what you've handed over to Him. Thank Him for being not only trustworthy but also loving. Thank Him that His ways are far better than your own. Finally, thank Him that He actually wants to enter into your life and have you be a part of His.

RECEIVE

_____, as you cling to your life, you will lose it; but if you give up your life for me, you will find it ... and you will experience life in the most fruitful and complete way! (Matthew 10:39 and John 10:10)

DAY 17
A HEART OF HUMILITY

There's a story about the great boxing champion, Joe Lewis, who was said to have the strength to put his fist through the side of a bull. One day, a rather brazen 10-year old boy actually picked a fight with Lewis on a bus, claiming that he could whip the champ. While Lewis graciously relented, the boy had no idea of the power he was encountering. And neither do we as we approach God. God is more than ready to go deeper in love with us, but that encounter will only happen if we humbly come to Him with the right perspective and position in relationship.

RE-POSITION

Here's one way to approach God humbly: before you come to Him, forgive or ask forgiveness from someone. Jesus, in telling His disciples what it really means to be in relationship with God, told them that it is an inside-out affair. Genuine heart posture matters more to God than right action with mixed motives. That is why Jesus says that before you offer who you are and what you have to Him, "first go and be reconciled to [those needing reconciliation with you]; then come and offer your gift" (Matthew 5:24).

To forgive or be forgiven takes a great amount of humility as we think more highly of others than we do ourselves. To have nothing in the way between you and others is to allow God to be God in your relationship and have nothing in the way of you and Him. Is there someone you need to forgive or ask forgiveness from? If so, take some time to pray, make a call, have a conversation, or whatever is needed so that peace may reign with you and others, and you and God.

RENEW

Spend some time with Jesus and think about all that He had to lay down and set aside in order to "become flesh and dwell among us." Talk about a humbling experience. As you contemplate all that Jesus rightly had coming to Him, thank Him for His willingness to lay it aside out of love for you. When you're done, take a few moments to let the following verse penetrate your heart and mind.

And being found in appearance as a man, he humbled himself by becoming obedient to death — even death on a cross! (Philippians 2:8)

FOOD FOR THOUGHT AND REFLECTION

"Now Moses was a very humble man, more humble than anyone else on the face of the earth," Numbers 12:3 tells us. Maybe you're not a Moses, but does humility mark your life? Is pride and arrogance becoming more and more distant in your rearview mirror? Are you laying down your desire to fight to be right, first, or have it your way? If so, you're on your way to a deeper intimacy with God. If not, it's time to begin, because in God's economy, a humble-hearted life is the only life.

God loves those who don't have it all put together and realize it. In fact, He actually shows favor to those who aren't know-it-alls and admit they have a long way to go and a lot to learn (Proverbs 3:34). God really isn't all that impressed with how much Scripture you can quote, what influential positions you might hold in your church, or even how many people you can notch on your spiritual belt as "saved." He is impressed, however, and pays great attention to the person who says, "Lord, have mercy on me, a sinner" (Luke 18:13) and "the few loaves and fish of my life don't seem to amount to much, but whatever I have, Lord, it's all yours." (John 6:5-12)

C.S. Lewis once said,
> *"True humility is not thinking less of yourself; it is thinking of yourself less." If Jesus humbled Himself from God's own Son to a nail-pierced man, from master of all to foot-washing servant, what posture of humility might you need to take that expresses how much you genuinely love Him? As with Jesus before the Father, when we "humble ourselves before the Lord, he will lift us up" (James 4:10).*

RESPOND

Are there any rights or privileges in your life, perceived or actual, that need surrendered in order to draw closer to God or to better live the life to which He has called you? Ask God to reveal such things to you and humbly lay them at His feet.

RECEIVE

Receive these truths from Scripture as you go:

If you exalt yourself, _____, you will be humbled; but if you humble yourself, you will be exalted. (Matthew 23:12)

When you are humble, _____, I will guide you in what is right and teach you in my way. (Psalm 25:9)

I mock proud mockers, but I show favor to the humble and oppressed. (Proverbs 3:34)

Humble yourself before me, _____, and I will lift you up. (James 4:10)

DAY 18
A HEART OF AUTHENTICITY

If jumping from a lakeside ledge, few would prefer to plunge their bodies into murky waters instead of jumping into transparent ones. Knowing what's beneath the surface makes the adventure so much more freeing, safe, and meaningful. So it is with love. Real love, deepening love, comes with authenticity.

◁▷

RE-POSITION

"Taste and see that the Lord is good," Psalm 34:8 tells us. God has created a connection from our taste buds to our souls! That's really no surprise—after all, as complete beings, God created us as a beautiful fusion of body, mind, and spirit. So grab a cup of coffee, a tall glass of iced tea, a cool cup of water, or some other beverage of choice and enjoy God for a moment or two. If a favorite snack is available, even better. Give thanks to God that He enjoys that you enjoy food and drink. Thank God for taste buds, for refreshing drinks, good food, and any other gift He graciously provides.

RENEW

A not-so-famous movie, *Innerspace* (1987), explored the idea of what it would be like if scientists could somehow be shrunk to miniscule proportions and journey the innermost caverns of the human body. All poorly written movies aside, imagine God, who can pull off such a scientific feat, traveling the landscape of your deepest thoughts, desires, and motivations. Ask Him to go deep, to have His way, and to reveal to you His findings.

Search me, God, and know my heart; test me and know my anxious thoughts. See if there is any offensive way in me, and lead me in the way everlasting. (Psalm 139:23-24)

FOOD FOR THOUGHT AND REFLECTION

How many people do you know who would truly say, "I crave falsehood, and inauthentic people are my favorite." To the contrary, we hear most often that honesty and authenticity are traits that draw us to others, traits admired, traits desired in ourselves as well as those around us.

Yet, to be honest, living in a genuine manner anywhere and everywhere is not as simple as longing for it to be so. It may be for many reasons, but the one main reason behind all of them is fear. We fear that our real selves are not valuable, worthy, lovable, likeable, or true. We fear, above all, that the One who created us in His image finds us undesirable. How can we possible exhibit transparency when we are hiding behind all manner of things so as not to be fully known?

The first step in living a life of authenticity is relinquishing our hiding places to the God who lovingly, wonderfully, and fearfully created us. If He knows our thoughts before we speak them, we need not keep them tucked away in fear when we spend time with Him. If the thoughts and hurts and emotions are difficult, if they are ugly, if they are full of doubt—do we think He can not handle them? Taking our entire selves out of hiding before our very Redeemer, Jesus Christ, is the beginning of the redemption we want so deeply.

Fostering a habit of bare authenticity in our relationship with God ushers in a truer, more fully alive version of who God created us to be—in our homes, in our churches, in our communities, in our work places, etc. The more we allow Him to search us and know us, the more we are transformed by His love for us, and the more we bear His image authentically.

RESPOND

Authenticity comes with vulnerability. We grow deeper in relationship with someone when we risk exposing things about ourselves that may not be received well. We dare to risk openness for a chance at deeper closeness. The key is trust. The more we trust that someone truly loves us genuinely, has our back, and accepts us "no matter what," the more we risk being vulnerable with that person.

God is trustworthy. He has your back. He loves you beyond measure. And He continues to love you no matter what you've done, where you've been, and where you've fallen short. Risk asking God for authenticity and healthy vulnerability with Him and others.

God honors authenticity. Listen for a while and write down whatever you hear (whether you think that it's directly from God or not). If you're in His presence, it's most likely God speaking in one form or another. It may be something that makes sense later. Regardless, whatever you genuinely sense or hear, write it down. The goal in this response and in all of your life with God is to allow "the real God to meet the real you" (C.S. Lewis).

RECEIVE

_____, you will seek me and find me when you seek me with all your heart (the good, the bad, the ugly). I already know you and the good plans I have for you (Jeremiah 29:13, 11).

So, _____, always come to Me just as you are ... I promise to send you away far better than you were!

DAY 19

A HEART OF CONFESSION AND FORGIVENESS

Nothing builds a dividing wall higher and more quickly in a relationship than failing to forgive or ask forgiveness. Like Adam and Eve in the garden, when we don't come clean with God and others, we hide from them, defend our position, and rationalize why life would be better off without them. God has a better and more life-giving way as we confess, forgive, and tear down the walls that keep us separated.

RE-POSITION

The Psalm-writer tells us that the only way to approach God is with "clean hands and a pure heart" (Psalm 24:4). If possible, have a bowl of water and a towel in front of you. Another option would be to go to a bathroom or kitchen sink. Your heart, and not the procedure, is the important thing here. As you bathe your hands in water, ask God to cleanse you and make you clean. Think about all that water does (cleanses, renews, refreshes, brings life, etc.) and how God does those things in you. Allow your prayer to be: "wash me, Lord, and I will be whiter than snow" (Psalm 51:7).

RENEW

Read through the following passage slowly and intentionally. Sit with it awhile. Allow these words of God to wash over you. After reading it through two or three times as such, listen. Share with God what you hear Him saying to you through the passage. Don't be in a hurry to get it done. When you sense it's time to move on in your time with God, do so with freedom and peace.

Restore to me the joy of your salvation and grant me a willing spirit, to sustain me. (Psalm 51:12)

FOOD FOR THOUGHT AND REFLECTION

God made things in such a way that they naturally sprout, grow, and have life. We marvel at the beauty of a wild field of flowers and how they seem to spring up all on their own. Consider children. Parents don't have to tell a young boy or girl to get bigger. They just feed them, and they physically mature all by themselves. Yes, God made things to grow all on their own, including our relationship with others and with Him. And grow they do, except ...

Except when barriers get in the way. For flowers, it may be weeds. For children, perhaps it's illness. For us with God, it's sin. Sin causes separation in relationship. Our desire to step outside of God's life-giving ways and choose another self-serving way hinders our growth with Him. In fact, it's worse. It actually causes damage and distances us from knowing Him in a deeper, more intimate way.

Do you remember what Adam and Eve did when they chose to do their own thing outside of God's design? They hid. They were also "afraid," Genesis 3 tells us. Hiding and afraid doesn't sound like very close intimacy, does it? That's what sin does.

But here's some good news. The Lord is "forgiving and good, abounding in love to all who call upon him" (Psalm 86:5). God actually makes Himself available when we distance ourselves from Him. He loves us that much.

King David struggled on more than one occasion to choose God's life-giving ways and precepts. Still, he was called "a man after God's own heart," because he loved God more than the distance he himself created. David prayed often, "against you only have I sinned ... create in me a clean heart ... renew a right spirit within me" (Psalm 51).

He discovered the truth the apostle John echoed centuries later, that "If we confess our sins, he who is faithful and just will forgive us our sins and cleanse us from all unrighteousness" (I John 1:9). Do you see it? As we agree with God and ask His forgiveness, our relationship becomes clean and the "rightness" of our love is restored. Now that sounds like an intimate, grow-all-on-its-own, life-giving relationship with God, doesn't it? As you are quick to confess the sin that separates you from God your intimacy with Him will continue to deepen.

RESPOND

Has God been speaking to you through His Spirit about some walls that are keeping you from deeper fellowship, joy, and intimacy with Him? Are there some things you just need to get on paper, some bricks that need to be named so that they can be taken down and eliminated?

Make a list of some of the bricks that are keeping you from right relationship with God and others. Who do you need to forgive? From whom do you need to ask forgiveness?

Ask God to "forgive your sin and cleanse you from all unrighteousness" (I John 1:9). Be aware that this is a daily and ongoing process in the life of one who grows deeper in love with God.

Make a list of "next steps" that God is leading you to in asking forgiveness from others and seeking to forgive.

RECEIVE

_____, as you have confessed your sin, know that I continue to be faithful and just, and I have absolutely cleansed you from all that comes between us. (I John 1:9)

Consider the bricks removed!

DAY 20
A HEART OF PATIENCE AND WAITING

"To learn patience is not to rebel against every hardship," Henri Nouwen once said. We become impatient when things get harder, move slower, or just aren't happening in the shape and fashion we hoped or imagined. Intimacy with God comes when we set aside all our expectations and allow His love to unfold as we wait patiently in love and trust.

RE-POSITION

Patience is called a virtue for a reason. It's not always easy to possess or practice. It's also something that is taught, not given. As you re-position yourself to come into God's presence today, do so by practicing patience. This can be done through the instrument of quietness and listening.

While you may be among the minority that can easily sit still and listen, most of us are "doers" by nature, and the thought of "being" quiet and still may seem somewhat like a waste of time; it seems counterproductive to the laundry list of things that awaits us at the conclusion of our time with God. That's the beauty of the lesson. We need to learn to wait, be still, and listen to the Lord. Some of us are more readily patient than others, and most of us know our tipping point when we begin to get fidgety and anxious in our waiting. That being so, do the following:

Wait as quietly and patiently upon God as you can tolerate. When you get to the point where it's really uncomfortable, wait some more … until you believe God releases you from your waiting. Ask God to keep your mind from wandering 10,000 different directions from all you have to do. Focus your waiting as much as you are able upon God—who He is, what He's done and doing. Ask Him to give you peace as He teaches you patience.

RENEW

Imagine being stuck in a deep pit, ensnared in a miry muck of mud (for most of us that isn't so hard to conceive). How long is worth waiting to hear from God, who will not only save you but lead you securely on your way?

I waited and waited and waited for God. At last he looked; finally he listened. He lifted me out of the ditch, pulled me from deep mud. He stood me up on a solid rock to make sure I wouldn't slip. (Psalm 40:1-3 The Message)

FOOD FOR THOUGHT AND REFLECTION

"Patience is waiting with kindness," a phrase created to help children grasp patience. It's tangible enough for little ones, especially when the waited-for thing is a turn on the swing or a cookie to come out of the oven. The grown-up definition may not be as simple.

Longsuffering. To suffer long. To patiently endure. This definition doesn't encourage us to "have a heart of patience." It adds salt to our wounds, to our waiting time.

If we aren't careful, all we are prone to hear about patience from the child definition or the grown-up definition is a pestering mockery. Patience is a learned posture that is not easy to master. When someone encourages us to "be patient," it does not feel encouraging, not to the child, the child in us, or the grown-up we're trying to become.

The hymn writer, Robert Robinson, prays, "Tune my heart to sing Thy grace." And with the same grace, we must tune our hearts to really hear what patience is ...

In Greek and Hebrew it is: to be of a long spirit, not to lose heart; to persevere patiently and bravely. Patience is to wait, to expect, to hope for.

Could it be that we can entrust our waiting to the kindness of Christ? Can we truly release the habit and craving for control of all of the little and big things and replace those with a hope for the Lord? What if there is rest in the heart of the Father, as He maintains a long spirit for us? What if He is waiting with kindness for us to abide in His safety, His sovereignty, His goodness? What a tremendous thought that the Father, Son, and Spirit persevere patiently and bravely for us.

Learning the posture of patience seems more attainable when we see God's patient posture toward us and for us.

RESPOND

Make a list of the places, people, and things that test your patience. For each item listed, ask God to teach you in His time and in His way.

Finish this sentence: Lord, my ability to wait patiently for you is most tested when …

Make a list of 4-5 ways that the Lord continues to be patient with you.

RECEIVE

I am not slow in keeping my promise, _____, as some understand slowness. Instead I am patient with you (and others), not wanting anyone to perish, but everyone to come to repentance. (2 Peter 3:9)

_____, I am a compassionate and gracious God, slow to anger, and abounding in love and faithfulness. (Psalm 86:15)

_____, the fruit of having my Spirit in you is a life of … patience. (Galatians 5:22)

_____, my love is patient. (1 Corinthians 13:4)

DAY 21
A HEART THAT EMBRACES SUFFERING AND TRIAL

As human beings, we fight against and avoid pain and suffering at just about any cost. Wisdom, however, tells us that our greatest times of growth and triumph come as we conquer difficult challenges, navigate painful situations, and rise above sorrowful circumstances. God actually uses the most tumultuous times of our lives to beckon us deeper into love, dependence, and intimacy with Him.

RE-POSITION

Sometimes the greatest way to gain right perspective with God is to begin thanking Him for all the "great things He has taught us, great things He has done," as one songwriter puts it. After settling yourself, simply make a list of ten things you are thankful for today. It doesn't have to be overly profound or spiritual. It could be as simple as thanking God for the goodness of your cup of coffee or that He allowed you to enjoy life yet another day. The point in all of this is to "raise your gaze" beyond yourself to the giver of all good gifts.

1.   6.
2.   7.
3.   8.
4.   9.
5.   10.

RENEW

A good way to encounter God in His Word is to focus on key words. In the following passage, circle any words that strike you as difficult, hopeful, challenging, or helpful. Write out each word you highlighted, and then write any thoughts and emotions those words provoke. Ask the Lord to bring insight to the truth His Word is uncovering.

Consider it pure joy, my brothers and sisters, whenever you face trials of many kinds, because you know that the testing of your faith produces perseverance. Let perseverance finish its work so that you may be mature and complete, not lacking anything. (James 1:2-4)

FOOD FOR THOUGHT AND REFLECTION

How do we make a conscious effort to consider real suffering "pure joy" when life is spinning at terrible speeds all around us, pain is throbbing in our temples in addition to our heart, and life's forecast is calling for turbulent winds and extended storms? Is it possible that we can somehow find joy beyond whatever pain, bafflement, and evil we might be facing on any given day or in any given season?

It is possible. In fact, we were made to trust and depend on God as the giver and sustainer of our life in all circumstances. One doesn't have to minimize the circumstance, deny reality, or otherwise mask whatever agony is at hand in order to paint a picture of a God who is good and supplies our every need.

Life is real, and hard, and at times, really, really painful. Hardship and suffering have been promised to us from the beginning. But an intimate relationship with God allows for rejoicing in a God of "refuge and strength" amid assaults, plots, and schemes (Psalm 62); singing at midnight when beaten and imprisoned (Acts 16:25); a blessedness when people insult you and go after your character (Matthew 5:11-12); and the centering assurance that because "the Lord is our shepherd," even walking in the valleys and shadows of death cannot separate us from a God who is ever with us (Psalm 23:4).

The call to "rejoice always, pray continually, and give thanks in all circumstances" (Thessalonians 5:16-18) is an honest expectation for the one who is willing to trust a God who sees the entirety of our lives in the view of eternity. He not only sees the big picture, He knows how to make sense of the heartaches, pitfalls, and tough terrain of our lives and lead us further in trusting and depending on Him. It's through leaning on and into God amid the most challenging and life-wrenching places that we, in time, rejoice and say "the Lord gives and takes away, blessed be the name of the Lord" (Ecclesiastes 1:21).

RESPOND

John 15:2 tells us, "He cuts off every branch in me that bears no fruit, while every branch that does bear fruit he prunes so that it will be even more fruitful." Make a list of the challenging and painful places, people, and relationships in your life. For each circumstance or situation, ask God to help you see His bigger plan in it all. Ask Him to teach you patience in the unknown and for strength to depend on Him each step of the way. Thank Him for His presence in your life and in the details of all your living.

RECEIVE

In the midst of whatever you may be facing, receive God's promises to walk with you each step of the way.

_____, I will NEVER leave you nor forsake you. (Joshua 1:5)

_____, my grace is sufficient for you, for my power is made perfect in weakness. (2 Corinthians 12:9)

Peace I leave with you; my peace I give you, _____. I do not give to you as the world gives. Do not let your heart be troubled and do not be afraid. (John 14:27)

WEEK 4
Fostering Love

Like any living thing that grows,
love requires nurture and care.
Love isn't something to be possessed
but fostered.
Love is so much more
than a single "yes" or "I do" at an altar,
but is a lifelong commitment
of daily choices and rhythms
that grows our relationship
with God from the inside-out.

DAY 22
A LIFE OF GRATITUDE

A thankful heart prepares the way for intimate love to grow. Gratefulness lifts one's eyes, thoughts, and desires far beyond the narrow scope of self to find contentment in what already is, was, and will be. Living with a rhythm of gratitude lovingly says to God and others, "you are enough."

RE-POSITION

Creativity is a wonderful gift of God. Today, as you begin to re-arrange your life and space to give God your full attention, let your imagination and your hands go to work. Draw or sketch something for which you're thankful. The drawing doesn't have to be professional, and the subject matter can be whatever is on your heart. If you are near dirt, sand, rocks, twigs, leaves, clay, etc., maybe you can use some of those elements in your creation. The idea is twofold: be thankful and give the best you have to offer to God.

If you're feeling that your "best" really isn't good enough for God, you're right—it never is, whether drawing or living. But that's the grace of God, isn't it? Our desire to please Him does, in fact, please Him—far beyond our ability to actually do so!

RENEW

Below, circle the words, "always" and "everything." Spend some time meditating on this passage. Ask God why He chose those two all-inclusive words. Be honest with God about the places in your life that might be challenged by an "always" and "everything" kind of gratitude.

. . . always give thanks to God the Father for everything, in the name of our Lord Jesus Christ. (Ephesians 5:20)

FOOD FOR THOUGHT AND REFLECTION

Gratitude is "happiness doubled by wonder," G.K. Chesterton says. Our gratitude radiates joy when we assess how much we graciously receive in any given situation, circumstance, or relationship compared to how little we actually give or deserve. That being so, perhaps no greater comparison of "who gets what" is worthy of gratitude than is our relationship with God. How can our hearts be anything but grateful when we marvel at all that God is doing and has done in us, around us, through us, beyond us, and even in spite of us. It's a "double-wonder" that makes our hearts glad indeed. When we have been given so much in an equation where our efforts alone merit us little to nothing, the only appropriate expression for us is a heart that overflows with thankfulness.

Is there anything that deepens a relationship faster than gratitude? Is there any better way to say "I love you" to God than to recognize and acknowledge all that He has lovingly, faithfully, and graciously done, and is doing, in and around us?

Tears often flow when an unearned check is received in the mailbox, a load of groceries is delivered to fill an empty pantry, a costly medical procedure is graciously donated, a heroic act is demonstrated, or another "make a wish" story is told. How much more should our hearts sing, our lips speak, and our bodies respond "to him who is able to do immeasurably more than all we ask or imagine"? (Ephesians 3:20). "Give thanks to the Lord, for he is good," Psalm 136 repeatedly reminds us, for "his love endures forever." And through our enduring thankfulness, our love for God grows deeper, closer, and sweeter.

RESPOND

A heart of thankfulness and the love of God go hand in hand. Interwoven twenty-six times in Psalm 136 is the enduring love of God and the psalm-writer's attempt to be thankful for the many ways God's love intersected and transformed his life.

Perhaps you can make a "thanks for loving me" list of your own. Take your time. Add to it later as things come to you throughout the day. Here's one to get you started:

Give thanks to the Lord … for He is good. His love endures forever.

RECEIVE

Receive this blessing as you join with others who have lived with grateful hearts before God:
Feel free to sing it if you know it!

Praise God, from whom all blessings flow;
Praise Him, all creatures here below;
Praise Him above, ye heavenly host;
Praise Father, Son, and Holy Ghost. Amen.

DAY 23
A LIFE OF WORSHIP

"Worship changes the worshiper into the image of the one worshiped," says author and pastor, Jack Hayford. That being so, perhaps we were meant for a life of transformational encounters far beyond one day a week or one hour each morning. We were created to live in a rhythm of daily worship where the echo of all of our being and doing proclaims, *"praise and glory and wisdom and thanks and honor and power and strength be to our God forever and ever. Amen!"* (Revelation 7:12).

RE-POSITION

Reading Scripture aloud is a great way to come into God's presence. Read the following passage aloud. Then, read it a second time, and make it personal. For example, "I praise you Lord. I praise you in your sanctuary." You get the idea. Feel free to lift your hands as well as your voice as you speak words of love and praise to God.

Praise the Lord. Praise God in his sanctuary; praise him in his mighty heavens. Praise him for his acts of power; praise him for his surpassing greatness. Praise him with the sounding of the trumpet, praise him with the harp and lyre, praise him with timbrel and dancing, praise him with the strings and pipe, praise him with the clash of cymbals, praise him with resounding cymbals. Let everything that has breath praise the Lord. Praise the Lord. (Psalm 150)

RENEW

God has blessed us with learning from and leaning on the collective wisdom of many who have come before us in our faith. Here are two different translations to compare regarding worship. Allow the Holy Spirit to provide connections that are as unique as you are as these passages resonate with you in different ways.

As you come to him, the living Stone — rejected by humans but chosen by God and precious to him — you also, like living stones, are being built into a spiritual house to be a holy priesthood, offering spiritual sacrifices acceptable to God through Jesus Christ. (1 Peter 2:4-5 NIV)

To change the metaphor, you come to him, as living stones to the immensely valuable living stone (which men rejected but God chose), to be built up into a spiritual House of God, in which you, like holy priests, can offer those spiritual sacrifices which are acceptable to God by Jesus Christ. (1 Peter 2:4-5 J. B. Phillips)

FOOD FOR THOUGHT AND REFLECTION

Marriage finds depth in long, steady years of "better's and worse's," not at the altar of "I do" on one's wedding day. And so it is in our relationship with Jesus. While committing one's life to Him is crucial in establishing a deeper love relationship with Him, it is the daily offering of oneself to His glory and pleasure that builds a deeper, lasting love. In the same manner that we would never expect a marriage to grow from a couple who said their vows and then spent the next twenty years simply living separate under the same roof, we should never expect that a weekly check-in at worship will grow our love relationship with Jesus by any significant degree. Our relationship with Jesus was intended as an abiding, "I in you—you in me," ongoing, love exchange, and that kind of love requires the daily devotion of one's heart every step of the way.

The writer of Romans tells us that the kind of worship we were really created for isn't just what takes place on Sundays, but is a continual—24/7, Monday through Saturday, heart and soul, mind and body, prayer and praise, thanksgiving and adoration, proclamation and response, loving God and neighbor—kind of worship exchange (Romans 12:1-2). To say it as plainly as possible: ALL of life is a time to worship!

So praise God in the kitchen, pray to Him at the copier, thank Him on the basketball court, offer yourself to Him at the coffee shop, adore Him on your date, ponder Him at the movies, sing to Him in the shower, commune with Him as you eat, proclaim Him as you study, acknowledge Him at the repair shop, and rest in Him as you relax. Whether sweating, sleeping, working, or playing—your life is a daily expression of love to God. So worship Him weekly with other believers—it's quite important. And then, continue your life of prayer and praise throughout the week as God daily deepens your love relationship with Him.

RESPOND

Take some time to think about your daily schedule. Would you say you live a life of worship throughout your day? How might you change things in thought, word, or deed in order to better live a life that sees worship as a 24/7 affair?

Consider each of the following life domains. Ask the Lord, "How can I better daily love and honor You through …?"

… my personal life?

… my family?

… my work or school?

… my church?

… my community and beyond?

RECEIVE

_____, I have loved you with an everlasting love; I have drawn you with unfailing kindness (Jeremiah 31:3). By day, My love is with you, at night I sing over you. (Psalm 42:8, paraphrased)

DAY 24
A LIFE IN COMMUNITY

No super heroes exist in the Christian life. We rejoice in community. We suffer in community. We rise and fall in community. Wherever you see someone accomplishing significant gains for God's Kingdom, rest assured they are living life together in intimacy and faith with God and others.

RE-POSITION

While God never changes His attitude toward us, we are much more fickle. Spending even a moderate amount of time with family and friends testifies to our up and down nature toward others. However you are feeling at this moment, list five reasons why meeting with God is worth it. Shifting the focus from our inconsistencies to His constancy almost always puts us in a better posture to meet with God.

RENEW

Read the following passage through once. Pause. Listen. Write down whatever you hear God saying.

Read through the passage a second time. This time, wherever you come across the words "they" and "everyone," substitute the word "we" (and any corresponding pronouns and verbs that make it read correctly). Again, pause, listen, and write down whatever you may hear God saying to you.

> They devoted themselves to the apostles' teaching and to fellowship, to the breaking of bread and to prayer. Everyone was filled with awe at the many wonders and signs performed by the apostles. All the believers were together and had everything in common. They sold property and possessions to give to anyone who had need. Every day they continued to meet together in the temple courts. They broke bread in their homes and ate together with glad and sincere hearts, praising God and enjoying the favor of all the people. And the Lord added to their number daily those who were being saved. (Acts 2:42-48)

FOOD FOR THOUGHT AND REFLECTION

Community is God's laboratory for love. Life together becomes the testing ground to see if what we say with our lips really makes its way to and from our heart. Saying that we love God rarely costs us anything, but demonstrating that in an arena of people who might question us, press us, frustrate us, challenge us, or even reject us is a whole other story. Love is a risky business, and knowing love to its fullest extent means sharing love in community.

Loving in community, however, isn't just about testing the full metal of our love. Community is meant to encourage love, celebrate love, and share love. God loves community, because as Father, Son, and Holy Spirit—He is community in the most perfect way. The psalmist describes the sweetness of love lived out in community: "how good and pleasant it is," he says, "it is like precious oil anointing one's head and flowing abundantly down one's face" (Psalm 133). The benefit of community is like "iron sharpening iron," the wisdom writer tells us (Proverbs 27:17).

Community isn't always easy. That's why so many shy away from it. But for those who dare to venture into its risky waters, as the first followers of Jesus did in the book of Acts (Acts 2:42-48), they find Jesus at the center, drawing the many uniquely made, differently wired, and ever-growing members toward Himself. As they discover a deeper love for Jesus, the community finds a deeper and more mature love for one another. And love grows. And love wins. And "by this," those who don't know God's never stopping, never giving up, un-breaking, always and forever love, will have no doubt knowing that God's love is for real (John 13:35).

RESPOND

As you compare your Christian community experience with that in Acts 2:42-48, ask God to show you how you might better live in love with others as you seek to live in love with Him.

Take a few minutes to call, text, or write a friend or two—whomever God puts on your mind. Take some time to encourage them. Thank them for being a part of your Kingdom journey with God.

RECEIVE

_____, it is so good and pleasant when I see you living together with God's people in unity! It's like precious oil poured on the head, running down on the beard, running down on Aaron's beard, down on the collar of his robe. It is as if the dew of Hermon were falling on Mount Zion. For there the LORD bestows His blessing, even life forevermore. Yes, _____, it's so sweet to see My people living in harmony. (Psalm 133, adapted)

DAY 25
A LIFE OF PRAYER

No greater conduit exists to know God and be known by Him than through prayer. Through prayer we acknowledge and practice the presence of God. And when God is near, we, and the things around us, change as we align our lives to His good, perfect, and pleasing will.

RE-POSITION

"Come to me … and I will give you rest," Jesus says to those wearied by life (Matthew 14:28). Rest may not seem particularly holy to you, but it may be the most spiritual thing you do today. Wherever you are on the "tired and weary" spectrum, take 3-5 minutes (longer if needed) and "rest" with God. If you're concerned about oversleeping, set an alarm. At the very least, breathe deeply and allow God's Spirit to calm your body, mind, and spirit. Ask God to renew you as He watches over your rest.

RENEW

Pray this simple prayer with great sincerity: "Lord, speak, you're servant is listening."

Rejoice always, pray continually, give thanks in all circumstances; for this is God's will for you in Christ Jesus.
(1 Thessalonians 5:16-18)

FOOD FOR THOUGHT AND REFLECTION

We don't understand a life of prayer. We often don't enter into prayer times, because we don't know how to, because we think it's supposed to look a certain way. Or we pray only at certain times, because that is prayer time, and everything else is not prayer time. I wonder if we don't understand a life of prayer because we have made it complicated and dutiful, specifically structured and unattainable.

What if we erase all of that and just start fresh, perhaps writing preconceived notions on a piece of paper then tearing them to shreds as a symbol of freeing ourselves from defeat in the area of prayer.

Praying simply involves talking to God. Sometimes when we are sitting still with God's Word and a journal, sometimes during quiet and sacred spaces. Sometimes when we're washing dishes or doing taxes, rocking a baby to sleep or taking a walk. Praying includes listening for God's voice. Sometimes when we are reading Scripture, sometimes as we are worshipping. Sometimes when we're at the grocery store, sometimes when we're playing basketball at the gym. Sometimes can be any time.

Jesus modeled an on-going conversation with His Father, as He told His followers that He did what the Father instructed Him to do (John 5:19). He also withdrew to quiet places to be alone in prayer (Luke 5:16). He modeled and expressed a very tender and yet bold manner in which we are to, and can, pray (Matthew 6:9-13).

The Lord's Prayer, as we have come to call it, is a beautiful place not only to begin to foster a thriving prayer journey, but it is a tremendous guide for practicing a lifestyle of prayer. We can learn, as we follow the example of Christ, that prayer is an integral piece of growing in intimacy with God.

RESPOND

Take some time to write a prayer to God. Simply put on paper what's going on in your heart and head. You can certainly write whatever you like, but here's a suggestion if you're feeling a bit stuck. It's the simple acronym "ACTS" (Adoration, Confession, Thanksgiving, Supplication). Below are some ways to help you start.

Adoration | Lord, I adore you because …

Confession | Lord, I confess to you that …

Thanksgiving | Lord, you are so good. Thank you for …

Supplication | Lord, some people and situations I want to bring to you are …

RECEIVE

_____, when you call to me, I will answer you and tell you great and unsearchable things you do not know. (Jeremiah 33:3)

DAY 26
A LIFE OF PRAISE

Praise is more than a duty to be fulfilled or a compliment that somehow makes God feel better about His worth. A life of praise enters into God's enjoyment of who He is and what He has done, is doing, and will do in His Kingdom and in your life. To praise God is to gain perspective from soaring heights that leads to growing roots of faith that run deep.

RE-POSITION

"The heavens declare the glories of God," proclaims the psalm writer (Psalm 19:1). A great way to change your perspective and re-position your attention is to raise your gaze beyond yourself and observe God's creation. As you view the vastness, beauty, and creative detail of God's design, praise God for who He is and what He's done far beyond how it effects you personally. For instance, "God, I praise you for the air you give to breathe and the colors that fill the sky."

RENEW

To "praise" is to "bless, exalt, extol, glorify, magnify, thank, and confess." In the deepest way, to praise God is to call attention to His glory, His weightiness, His altogether otherness. As you read the following passage, make it personal, something like, "I praise you, Lord, everything within me praises you ... I praise your holy name." As you praise God, allow His presence to accompany you.

Praise the Lord, my soul; all my inmost being, praise his holy name. (Psalm 103:1)

FOOD FOR THOUGHT AND REFLECTION

"Praise the Lord!" It rolls off our tongues very easily, and sometimes casually, sometimes without thought, sometimes without meaning what we really say.

What does it really mean to praise the Lord, to live a life of praise? Can we do it? Can we live a story of authentic and on-going praise?

Several words are used for praise in both the Old and New Testaments, and the definitions include what we might think: give laud, thanksgiving, praise; boasting about, sing a song of praise. We may not expect that other sorts of definitions are included: shine a light upon, to confess, to shoot or throw down, to offer a sacrifice of praise, a thing belonging to God or Christ. Throughout the string of words woven as God's story revealed through Scripture, praise pours forth in both times of rejoicing and in times of hardship, both in times of asking for victory before a battle and in the midst of the battle itself.

Practically speaking, our lives are to bear forth praise—to shine a light upon God. When times are challenging, let us confess that He is worthy of our praise. When times are mediocre, let us offer thanks anyway for all of the glorious ways that God has provided for us and has shown Himself trustworthy throughout the course of our lives. When we are pressed in and pushed down, let us shoot our words of boasting about God into the darkness and know that the enemy can't stand our choice of weapons. When we are weary, may we lay a sacrifice of praise before God and trust that we can rest in Him.

Our very lives belong to God through Christ. Our words, songs, actions of praise—whether audible to those around us or only audible to God at times of private prayer—also belong to Him.

RESPOND

Revelation 4:8 describes heavenly hosts praising God day and night with a never stopping anthem of "Holy, holy, holy is the Lord God Almighty, who was, and is, and is to come." What does it look like for you to live a life of constant praise?

Take some time to give God praise in this moment. Whether or not you would consider yourself a good singer, let all that is within you put God on display as you sing:

> *Holy, holy, holy! Lord God Almighty!*
> *Early in the morning our song shall rise to thee.*
> *Holy, holy, holy! Merciful and mighty,*
> *God in three persons, blessed Trinity!*
>
> *Holy, holy, holy! All the saints adore thee,*
> *casting down their golden crowns around the glassy sea;*
> *cherubim and seraphim falling down before thee,*
> *which wert, and art, and evermore shalt be.*
>
> *Holy, holy, holy! Though the darkness hide thee,*
> *though the eye of sinful man thy glory may not see,*
> *only thou art holy; there is none beside thee,*
> *perfect in power, in love and purity.*
>
> *Holy, holy, holy! Lord God Almighty!*
> *All thy works shall praise thy name, in earth and sky and sea.*
> *Holy, holy, holy! Merciful and mighty,*
> *God in three persons, blessed Trinity.*

("Holy, Holy, Holy! Lord God Almighty," Text: Reginald Heber (1826), Music: John B. Dykes)

RECEIVE

_____, as you have blessed Me, so I bless you. Know that I am keeping you. My face shines upon you, and My grace, it covers you. My attention and presence is turned toward you. May you know and experience My peace. (Numbers 6:24-26, adapted)

DAY 27
A LIFE IN THE WORD

Like prayer and praise, a life in the Word gets up-close and personal with God in quick fashion. It does so, because God's Word is indeed God's words — a personal disclosure from His heart to yours regarding His nature, His plan, His desires, and His ways. What could ever draw you closer to the heart of God than a love letter penned by Him, written specifically to you?

RE-POSITION

God's voice calling us through His Word often moves us from our itinerary to God's better agenda. Take some time to read, and then pray, these words from God to you.

Give all your worries and cares to God, for he cares about you.
(1 Peter 5:7, New Living Translation)

Come close to God, and God will come close to you.
(James 4:8, New Living Translation)

Personalize these passages and make them your prayer …

> *"Lord, I give you all my anxieties. Thank You for caring for me so much that you gladly take them."*

> *"Lord, here I am. I want to be close to You. Please come close to me."*

RENEW

If possible, find a room with no windows or light. If that's not feasible, simply close or cover your eyes so that, as much as possible, you experience darkness. Imagine a life without light. Those who have poor vision or are blind know this reality well and will have less need of imagining. What might you stumble into? Where might you lose your way? How might living only in darkness change the way you function on a daily basis? In that frame of mind, meditate on the significance of the following passage:

Your word is a lamp for my feet, a light on my path.
(Psalm 119: 105)

FOOD FOR THOUGHT AND REFLECTION

In today's culture, reading material and consuming information of all sorts is in no short supply. Daily devotionals, online and hardbound commentaries, blogosphere communities with streams of comments and opinions—we don't have to look past the ends of our fingers to find words for our lives.

What would happen, just suppose, if we put some of those resources aside for a little while and began to allow God's Word—His words to us and for us—to read us? Knowing and being known is a goodly portion of what a life in Scripture looks like and what will expose our hearts repeatedly to God's transformative and on-going love story.

That may be helpful information, but it begs a very pragmatic response of, "Okay, thank you. So what does that mean for me in very tangible terms?" How about 10-20 minutes. A Bible. A quiet space like in a car, a lunch break beginning, a stairwell, a park bench, or the rocking chair in your child's room while you listen to them sleep. How about a simple, honest prayer:

"God, open your Word to me. If something is illumined and I hear from You, thank you. If I sit with the words on the page, and the quiet echoes back to me, I trust You with the stillness to do something in my heart anyway."

How about engaging daily. For an experiment, sincerely lay aside the endless stream of words that are constantly available through the interweb. Allow God to meet you as you engage Him through Scripture, just you and the Living God.

Choose to be a bit counter-cultural. Choose to take God up on His promise that as we draw near to Him, He will draw near to us. Choose to foster a life in the Word.

RESPOND

Instead of listening to what everyone else has to say about God … why don't you let Him speak for Himself in His own words. Ask God to direct you to a passage that He wants to share with you. If you hear nothing, pick a passage on your own. Ask God to meet you where you are and speak in ways you need to understand. He will be faithful to meet you.

Take a few moments to memorize Psalm 119:105: "Your word is a lamp for my feet, a light on my path." Put it to memory, not so that you can demonstrate how much you know about God, but that God can remind you how much He knows about you! Ask God to bring the verse to mind throughout your day and to teach and guide you with its truth.

RECEIVE

Receive the blessing of those who have come before you and are cheering you on as you run the race of faith and love:

For this reason, since the day we heard about you, _____, we have not stopped praying for you. We continually ask God to fill you with the knowledge of his will through all the wisdom and understanding that the Spirit gives, so that you may live a life worthy of the Lord and please him in every way: bearing fruit in every good work, growing in the knowledge of God, being strengthened with all power according to his glorious might so that you may have great endurance and patience, and giving joyful thanks to the Father, who has qualified you to share in the inheritance of his holy people in the kingdom of light. For he has rescued us from the dominion of darkness and brought us into the kingdom of the Son he loves, in whom we have redemption, the forgiveness of sins. (Colossians 1:9-14)

DAY 28
A LIFE OF GENEROSITY

Unlike most of the world around us, a life of generosity lives by the mantra: "What's in this for you!" God has nothing to gain by giving us anything. It's just the way He is — generous. And as we continue to reflect God's heart of generosity, our love for Him is deepened as we become more like Him.

RE-POSITION

Sometimes the prayers of others place the words in our heart that we long to speak but cannot quite formulate. Here's a prayer from the heart of Thomas Merton that might help you turn your gaze more fully toward God today:

> *"My Lord God, I have no idea where I am going. I do not see the road ahead of me. I cannot know for certain where it will end. Nor do I really know myself, and the fact that I think that I am following your will does not mean that I am actually doing so. But I believe that the desire to please you does in fact please you. And I hope I have that desire in all that I am doing. I hope that I will never do anything apart from that desire. And I know that if I do this you will lead me by the right road though I may know nothing about it. Therefore will I trust you always though I may seem to be lost and in the shadow of death. I will not fear, for you are ever with me, and you will never leave me to face my perils alone." (Thomas Merton, Thoughts in Solitude)*

RENEW

As you read, note what the benefits are in having a heart that resembles God's. Make a list of the rewards of being generous as God is generous.

Remember this: Whoever sows sparingly will also reap sparingly, and whoever sows generously will also reap generously. Each of you should give what you have decided in your heart to give, not reluctantly or under compulsion, for God loves a cheerful giver. And God is able to bless you abundantly, so that in all things at all times, having all that you need, you will abound in every good work. (2 Corinthians 9:6-8)

FOOD FOR THOUGHT AND REFLECTION

God is a giver. His generosity is beyond measure. He freely gave us the mountains and the seas, the sky and the land, and everything in between that helps bring life, sustain life, and enjoy life. What's more, He gave us Himself. In the beginning, He spoke us into existence, breathed His very life into our nostrils, and called us "very good." God gifted all of this to us without one ounce of effort or merit on our part. A loving gift from a generous God—"just because."

But God's generosity goes even further. The truth is, we took His gift and discarded it when the shine wore off. In our selfishness we said, "thanks, but no thanks," to God. "Nice effort, God, but we believe we can do better on our own." Yet, even in our arrogance God remained charitable toward us—"compassionate and gracious, slow to anger, and abounding in love and faithfulness" (Psalm 86:15).

The fullest expression of God's generosity came in the gift of Jesus—God with us. Jesus graciously set aside His rightful entitlements as "God of very God," and generously moved into our messy lives and neighborhoods to renew a love relationship with the Father that we ourselves destroyed.

That's the heart of a gracious and generous God. He calls us to the same. "Freely you have received ..." Jesus said to His disciples as they headed out to tell people about a Kingdom where real love and generosity flow, "... freely give" (Matthew 10:8). Do you want to know God in a deeper way? Be generous as He is generous. Be generous with your love, your time, your money, your appreciation, your compliments, your understanding, your patience, your forgiveness, etc. "God loves a cheerful giver" (2 Corinthians 9:7). So give! And allow your heart to feel the joy of a generous God as you do.

RESPOND

Matthew 10:8 says, "freely you have received, freely give." Practice generosity today by cheerfully giving something to someone "just because." Ask God what that "something" to give is and who to give it to. If possible, do it anonymously. Allow God to be the one who thanks and blesses you.

If God so moves and/or you so desire, make a week of it. Ask God for things to give and for people to give things to. Ask Him to make your heart more generous like His.

RECEIVE

_____, remember this: if you sow sparingly, you will also reap sparingly, and if you sow generously, you will also reap generously. Give what you have decided in your heart to give, not reluctantly or under compulsion, because I love a cheerful giver. And I am able to bless you abundantly, so that in all things at all times, having all that you need, you will abound in every good work. (2 Corinthians 9:6-8)

Know this too, _____, give, and it will be given to you. A good measure, pressed down, shaken together and running over, will be poured into your lap. For with the measure you use, it will be measured to you. (Luke 6:38)

WEEK 5
Walking in Love

*Love in its fullest expression is
not something to be hoarded but shared.
God's story continues to be written both
in you and through you.
While the benefit of knowing God intimately is great,
we only know the fullness of that love when
we walk with God in daily loving others.
In God's great love story, love isn't fully love
until it's given away.*

DAY 29
WALKING IN THE LOVE OF GOD

Perhaps you've heard the expression, "He's walking with a new skip in his step," or the one that goes, "She's dancing to a new tune." If so, you have a greater insight into what it is like to be more in love with God. It is a love that changes the way you move and relate on a daily basis. And it comes with a warning label: contagious.

RE-POSITION

Here's a simple idea of coming into God's presence in an all-attentive way. Consider the lyrics to the chorus of a well-known children's song, "Jesus Loves Me." Sing the song once or twice through and allow the words to begin to settle within your spirit.

Then, actually speak the lyrics. Own what the words say. Be thankful it is true. Be sure to express to God how you feel about Him as well:

"Yes, Jesus loves me!"

RENEW

Ask God to meet you beyond what human understanding and logic can provide. Express your willingness to open yourself up to all He has for you. Acknowledge that while such openness comes with risk, you will trust Him as He leads.

And I pray that you, being rooted and established in love, may have power, together with all the Lord's holy people, to grasp how wide and long and high and deep is the love of Christ, and to know this love that surpasses knowledge — that you may be filled to the measure of all the fullness of God. (Ephesians 3: 17-19)

FOOD FOR THOUGHT AND REFLECTION

As we fall into step with the Father, walking daily close by His side, we recognize His voice more readily. Our senses are more keenly in touch with His Spirit. Also noticeable are the various alluring, and sometimes subtle, voices that call to us and wish for us to walk under a different banner, something other than the love of God.

It is a paradox. No doubt, walking intimately with God won't be done accidentally, nor will it happen without a bit of a tussle with our own thoughts and the voices of the world that vie for our attention. Abiding in His love, staying close to His side, draws our hearts ever closer to His heart; staying in that place of safety and assurance comes with the price of losing all of the other banners under which we have walked in the past.

No longer unworthy, God's love says we are worthy.

No longer ashamed, God's love declares us new.

No longer a liar, God's love calls us to Truth.

No longer an addict, God's love beckons us forward as those who overcome in Christ.

No longer abandoned, God's love marks us as chosen and adopted ones.

No longer rejected, no longer outcast, God's love says, "You are mine."

No longer needy, God's love fills us to overflowing.

No longer controlling, God's love lets us trust His lead and His provision.

No longer afraid, God's love rescues and protects.

No longer are we defined or driven by old titles, old sins, old wounds, old idols. God's love—so high, so deep, so long, so wide—changes everything. As we learn from Jesus, this gentle and humble shepherd, even the way we walk is changed.

RESPOND

Ephesians 5:2 says, "walk in the way of love, just as Christ loved us and gave himself up for us as a fragrant offering and sacrifice to God."

What does it mean for you to "walk in love"?

How might your life need to take on a new shape or pattern to make a lifestyle of love more evident?

What might you need to lay down or pick up for that to begin to happen?

RECEIVE

_____, it gives Me great joy when I see you walking in the truth, just as the Father commanded. Here's a truth that's been around from the beginning: Love one another. And this is love: walk in obedience to what I tell you. From the very beginning, what I have asked of you and modeled for you is that you walk in love. (2 John 1:4-6, adapted)

DAY 30
WALKING WITH THE EYES OF GOD

What if you saw all that God sees? It might overwhelm you and break your heart. Equally, it might put you in a position for His restoring and beautifying love to be passed on to others. Intimacy with God gives us keener vision to see what God sees ... and respond.

RE-POSITION

Music has a great way of opening one's heart and mind to what God is saying and doing. St. Augustine once said, "to sing once is to pray twice." Here's an old hymn that might help in that process. If you know it, sing. If the song and tune are unfamiliar, let the poetry of the piece become your melody as you make this your prayer:

> *Open my eyes, that I may see*
> *glimpses of truth thou hast for me;*
> *place in my hands the wonderful key*
> *that shall unclasp and set me free.*
> *Silently now I wait for thee,*
> *ready, my God, thy will to see.*
> *Open my eyes, illumine me, Spirit divine!*

"Open My Eyes, That I May See," Words & Music: Clara H. Scott, 1895

RENEW

David asked, "Search me, God, and know my heart" (Psalm 139:23). As you read the following passage, will you do the same? Give God an open invitation to inspect the caverns of your heart. Ask Him to show you the places that need His loving attention.

The Lord does not look at the things people look at. People look at the outward appearance, but the Lord looks at the heart.
(1 Samuel 16:7)

FOOD FOR THOUGHT AND REFLECTION

A young boy longs to visit the Grand Canyon. He's seen pictures in his school books and pamphlets from the library. He's read what he can to try and understand what it means that there is a huge gaping canyon stretched across miles and miles. He has asked so many questions to piece together this grand thing. One day, his father surprises him with news that the family would be taking a trip in the summer, and finally, the boy was going to have his chance to see with his own eyes what pictures had tried to convey.

On the day of the actual visit—not just to the state and to the region, but the actual visit to the very specific rim of the edge of the Grand Canyon—the boy and his family met with a guide, an older gentleman who was an expert on this natural wonder. The boy was overwhelmed and a bit breathless at just one glance. No photograph could have prepared him for the sight of the canyon, for the vastness of the ravine, for the amount of details he saw in the overall formation and in the minutest of details along the trails they walked. He soaked in every moment, savoring the shapes and sounds and the birds and other types of wildlife, and the way the sky didn't even look the same from this place. He never imagined that he would be seeing everything.

This is how it is when we walk intimately with the Lord. The more we walk closely with Him, the more purposeful we are about letting Him lead us, the more vividly we see everything. People look different, for we see them as they were intended to be seen. Creation all around us appears with some kind of sharpened clarity. When we look in the mirror, we see ourselves more fully. Our eyes are changed, because seeing with God's eyes changes everything.

RESPOND

Be intentional today to go where other people are—work, school, a shopping area, a park, etc. Any place where people are will do. You don't need to speak to anyone, just observe. What's going on with the people you see? What might they be thinking, feeling, discerning, rejoicing over, worrying about, grieving over, or struggling with? Ask God to help you to see them as He does. Ask Him to break your heart for what breaks His.

Take time to pray for the people you observe. And, if God leads, respond in whatever way He prompts you.

RECEIVE

_____, I do not look at the things that other people look at when they see you. People look at your outward appearance, but I look at your heart. (1 Samuel 16:7, paraphrased)

DAY 31
WALKING WITH GOD IN THE ORDINARY

God is equally present in the cafeteria as He is the cathedral. In fact, here's one better: God is present everywhere you go and in everything you do. He's the God who makes Himself known to "whosoevers" in here, there, and everywhere places through everyday, ordinary people just like you.

◁▷

RE-POSITION

Spend some time catching up with God over a cup of coffee, tea, or another favorite beverage of choice. Tell Him how your day has gone so far, what you've been up to lately, about something interesting or perplexing you saw on the internet or read in a book, how your favorite sports team is doing, a favorite meal you've had lately, etc. Be sure to take some time to ask God how things are going with Him.

RENEW

Take a walk with Jesus in the places He goes. Imagine walking alongside Jesus in the crowd. What do the places He visits look like? Who does He stop and see? Who does He pass by? What emotions and attitudes surround those He sees before His visit and then after? As you walk along with Jesus, allow Him to bring faces, scents, conversations, and encounters to life.

Jesus went through all the towns and villages, teaching in their synagogues, proclaiming the good news of the kingdom and healing every disease and sickness. (Matthew 9:35)

FOOD FOR THOUGHT AND REFLECTION

If you're serious about getting up close to Jesus, you're going to have to go where Jesus is. While you'll most likely see Him at church on Sunday, that's not where He spends most of His time. You're going to have to try catching up with Him in some other places—like the grocery store, the office, the gym, the movie theater, or the restaurant. If you don't see Him there, try the neighbor's yard, the local mall, the soccer game, or the gas station. Jesus will be where people are—all kinds of people. But you need not look far, because Jesus will be wherever you are in your everyday, ordinary places. He wants to walk with you, as together you love those you encounter on a daily basis.

In Mark 6 we see a beautiful picture of Jesus going to His hometown, to numerous nearby villages, to a remote hillside, and even to the middle of a lake—all to be present with people who were in need of a restoring touch of body, mind, or soul. In the book of Acts (3:6), it's "along the way" that Peter and John offer Jesus' healing power to a crippled man. Jesus' promise "to be with them always" (Mt 28:20) held true.

And Jesus' promise holds true for you too. He wants to be with you and love others through you in the places and spaces you find yourself on a daily basis. Is there anything that deepens a relationship more than spending time together as you do things that matter?

RESPOND

Here's an ordinary thing: bread. Simple, yet profound. So extraordinary was this ordinary commodity that Jesus saw fit to use it to help us remember His body broken for us on the cross and to depend upon Him for ongoing provision as we pray for "daily bread." If you have access to some bread, get a piece and set it in front of you. If you don't have bread around, no worries whatsoever—just use another ordinary thing, perhaps your hands. Whether bread, hands, or something else you consider ordinary, take some time to study the everyday nature of what you have before you. Consider all the ways it comes into contact with others, how it satisfies vital daily needs, how it often goes unnoticed but would be greatly missed if absent.

Now take a moment to consider some ways your life may seem quite ordinary to you. Equally, take some time to think about all the places you go, people you connect with, and things you do that could become extraordinary means for God to reach others.

Ask God to help you see the extraordinary power of your ordinary life. Like loaves and fishes, offer to God whatever you have and allow Him to do with you whatever He desires as He feeds the masses.

RECEIVE

_____, I can do anything, you know — far more than you could ever imagine or guess or request in your wildest dreams! I do it, not by pushing you around, but by working deeply and gently within you through My Spirit. All for the purpose of proclaiming:

Glory to God in the church!
Glory to God in the Messiah, in Jesus!
Glory down all the generations!
Glory through all millennia! Oh, yes!

(Ephesians 3:20-21, The Message, adapted)

DAY 32
WALKING WITH GOD IN RISKY PLACES

To love much, we risk much. Like gold tested in a fiery furnace, our love for God often shows its true metal in the crucible of life. As our passion for God increases, so does our willingness to love in hard, messy, and sometimes dangerous places. Intimacy with God often takes us where only real love is willing to travel.

RE-POSITION

On a scale of 1-10, where are you with God today? Do you feel distant, close, ambivalent, apathetic, fearful, stressed, anxious, energized, alive? Wherever you are and whatever you're feeling, tell God about it. You may want to write your thoughts on paper and symbolically lay it at His feet. However you express it, may your heart's desire be: "Lord, here's all of me—just as I am. Do with me what you will!"

RENEW

Ask God to illumine your heart and mind as you read the passage below. Ask the Lord, "What do You want me to see here? What do You want me to know or learn?"

The third time he said to him, "Simon son of John, do you love me?"

Peter was hurt because Jesus asked him the third time, "Do you love me?" He said, "Lord, you know all things; you know that I love you."

Jesus said, "Feed my sheep. Very truly I tell you, when you were younger you dressed yourself and went where you wanted; but when you are old you will stretch out your hands, and someone else will dress you and lead you where you do not want to go." Jesus said this to indicate the kind of death by which Peter would glorify God. Then he said to him, "Follow me!" (John 21: 17-19)

FOOD FOR THOUGHT AND REFLECTION

Passion is a willingness to suffer for that which you hold dear. One who is passionate about ballet willingly endures strenuous workouts, endless choreographic repetition, and sore joints—all for the love of dancing. Someone impassioned about hungry children eagerly volunteers long hours, gives generous financial gifts, and perhaps even travels to remote countries and hard to get to places—all to help children live and not die. Passion comes with a price tag, a readiness to back up one's talk with action, no matter the cost. If you ever want to know how passionate someone is about something, see how much they are willing to suffer and sacrifice for it.

How passionate are you about Jesus? How passionate do you want to be? Are you willing to go wherever, and do whatever, He asks? Are you prepared to lay down or pick up whatever He requests?

Peter, as passionate a person as they come, struggled with his passion when put to the test. He said he loved Jesus, but when push came to shove, Peter denied Jesus, not once, but three times. He wasn't sure what aligning himself with Jesus would mean, so he played it safe.

We understand, many of us cash checks with our mouths that our lives don't cover. In time, Peter discovered what Jesus taught about early in their adventure together—that there's a blessedness when people "insult you, persecute you and falsely say all kinds of evil against you" because of your relationship with Him (Matthew 5:14). Our willingness to go to the sometimes tough and dangerous places with Jesus, not only draws others to the very love of God, but it also deepens our relationship with Him.

RESPOND

In John 21, for each of Peter's three denials, Jesus had a healing and restoring response. Do you have some denials that need restored? Are there places you have said with your lips that you love Jesus, but out of fear and comfort have denied responding to Jesus' call to "follow me" and "feed my sheep"? If so, confess those denials to Jesus and allow Him to restore you with His forgiveness and grace.

What might be your greatest fear(s) if God called you to places and people you consider risky?

Take some time to be still and listen. Is God tugging at your heart? Is there a gnawing in your gut? Is He calling you beyond comfort, control, and fear? If so, talk to Him about it, and write down whatever you hear Him saying.

If God has spoken to you about risky place kind of love; tell someone, and take a next step.

RECEIVE

_____, come, follow me, and I will show you how to fish for people! (Matthew 4:19, NLT)

_____, I am with you always, to the very end of the age. (Matthew 28:20)

_____, I have not given you a spirit of fear, but of power and of love and of a sound mind. (2 Timothy 1:7, NKJV)

WALKING WITH AN OVERFLOWING HEART

"The greatest gift you will ever give the world," says Forge's founder and president, Dwight Robertson, "is your intimacy with God." Love is not something burdensome that you have to muster up, but is something that is poured out as God continues to fill you to overflowing.

RE-POSITION

The concerns that most often fill the capacity of our heart and mind are usually the things that we care about the least. Work projects, grocery lists, bills to write, calendars and schedules, etc., have a way of occupying our attention and become distracting, if not overwhelming, as we seek to give God our undivided attention. As you begin today, why not reverse the order of things that hold your interest?

Take some deep breaths and begin to relax. As undesired cares and concerns surface in your mind, offer them to God. As good or important as any of them may be, express to God that He is the "greater portion" for you in these moments (Luke 10:42). If it is helpful, make a list of the "lesser things" to pick up later.

RENEW

Before you read, genuinely pray: "If it pleases you, speak, Lord. What You have to say is always worth hearing. Please give me ears to hear."

A good man brings good things out of the good stored up in his heart, and an evil man brings evil things out of the evil stored up in his heart. For the mouth speaks what the heart is full of. (Luke 6:45)

FOOD FOR THOUGHT AND REFLECTION

Our hearts are always overflowing. Catch someone on any given day in the middle of a particular task or situation, and you will see the overflow of their heart. For better or for worse, or for mediocre, what is in the depths of us will spill out into the way we live, the way we talk, the way we think. The beautiful news tucked inside the good news of the gospel is that life with God through Christ does transform our hearts.

It is worth noting that we are on a journey, we are traveling a road toward something more full, more complete. The author and finisher of our faith is constantly writing our stories and bringing our faith to maturity. There are days when what pours out just isn't very lovely; perhaps it is downright gross. Or maybe what seeps out is full of sadness that leaves us wrecked and questioning our faith. It's okay. Take a deep breath. Remember that you are in process, that you are still growing and changing. Truth be told, we are not fully engaging with God if we aren't allowing the Holy Spirit to diligently teach and correct us on the ugly overflow days. While we may desire lovely things to always be pumping from our heart, we know that just isn't so this side of heaven. We need to allow God to meet us in all the conditions of our overflowing heart. God honors hearts that overflow honestly.

As we travel the road, what flows out of us will more and more consistently resemble fruit that looks like Jesus. A driving habit of intimate, on-going conversation with the Lord changes us from the inside out. What is on the inside manifests and flows out. A heart that is yielded to the transformative power of Christ is a heart that overflows with a beauty, a hope, and a deep joy that spills out a beautiful fragrance.

If it is helpful, go back and re-visit Day 5 ("A God Who Knows You Intimately"), Day 9 ("A Story With a Past, Present, and Future"), Day 18 ("A Heart of Authenticity"), and Day 19 ("A Heart of Confession and Forgiveness").

RESPOND

Consider what words come out of your mouth. This isn't about cussing and such, but about what occupies the approximate 7,000-20,000 words that men and women respectively speak per day. What do the subjects that fill your speech say about what is at the depths of your heart?

Is sharing about your relationship with Jesus burdensome to you and does it make you anxious? Does sharing about other significant relationships in your life (spouse, child, parent, friend) or things like sports, food, fashion, hobbies, etc., make you feel the same? If not, why not? Is it possible that Jesus doesn't quite fill the capacity and passion of your heart quite as much as you think? Talk to God about this matter. Ask Him to put things in proper order and perspective.

Even with the best of intentions, our relationship with God can turn to wearisome religious activity in a hurry. We were not meant for a life that flows from an empty spirit. Ask God to create in you a clean heart and to renew a right spirit within you, so that the joy of His salvation might be restored and evident in all you say and do (Psalm 51:10-12).

RECEIVE

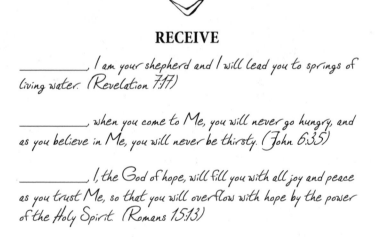

_____, I am your shepherd and I will lead you to springs of living water. (Revelation 7:17)

_____, when you come to Me, you will never go hungry, and as you believe in Me, you will never be thirsty. (John 6:35)

_____, I, the God of hope, will fill you with all joy and peace as you trust Me, so that you will overflow with hope by the power of the Holy Spirit. (Romans 15:13)

DAY 34
WALKING TO SEE, STOP, SPEND TIME WITH

When we love as Jesus loves, we do what Jesus did. As God's love in us matures, we more readily see where God is at work around us and follow the loving in-ear instruction of the Holy Spirit.

RE-POSITION

If possible, go on another walk with God. If that is not feasible, your current location is fine. Have no agenda outside of acknowledging that God is with you and you are with Him. If He speaks, great—listen. If He seems silent, that's okay too—trust His promise that He is always with you (Matthew 28:20). As it seems good to God and you, continue your time together.

RENEW

After reading the story below, take some time to enter into it. Close your eyes and allow imagination to do its work. For just a few moments, become Bartimaeus. What does it feel like to be blind and without hope? What is like to be ignored by everyone else but noticed by Jesus? Use all of your senses—allow God to take you from Bartimaeus' story to your own as Jesus asks you, "What is it you want Me to do for you?"

> Then they came to Jericho. As Jesus and his disciples, together with a large crowd, were leaving the city, a blind man, Bartimaeus (which means "son of Timaeus"), was sitting by the roadside begging. When he heard that it was Jesus of Nazareth, he began to shout, "Jesus, Son of David, have mercy on me!" Many rebuked him and told him to be quiet, but he shouted all the more, "Son of David, have mercy on me!" Jesus stopped and said, "Call him." So they called to the blind man, "Cheer up! On your feet! He's calling you." Throwing his cloak aside, he jumped to his feet and came to Jesus. "What do you want me to do for you?" Jesus asked him. The blind man said, "Rabbi, I want to see." "Go," said Jesus, "your faith has healed you." Immediately he received his sight and followed Jesus along the road. (Mark 10:46-52)

FOOD FOR THOUGHT AND REFLECTION

The famous line, "I see dead people," from the 1999 movie thriller, *The Sixth Sense*, became an instant catchphrase. The idea behind the movie's title was that some people have the rare ability to see things and people that no one else notices. Their perception becomes a "sixth sense."

Jesus had such a sense. His perception of people and things around Him were astonishingly above the ordinary. He sensed and saw things going on around Him like no one else in history ever has. He saw the overlooked, the undervalued, the burdened, the broken, the hurting, and yes, the dead and dying.

But Jesus didn't just see. He also stopped and spent time with those He knew needed a deeper touch of the Father. He not only noticed their lives, He also entered into their lives. His compassion moved Him to action.

As we walk with God, His love calls us to stop and spend time with people that He helps us to see. And here's the good news—the deeper we are in love with Jesus, the better we see. "You will do greater things than these," Jesus said to His disciples (John 14:12). That means He will give you what is needed to see the people all around you in your ordinary, everyday places. He will also provide the courage required to connect them to the Father's unfathomable love and healing power.

What might your life look like if you daily walked with Jesus to all the places you go? What if He whispered, "there's one, stop a moment with him" or "there's another, take some time with her"? Well, that's exactly what He does. And as we see, stop, and spend time with those Jesus brings our way, our love deepens as we depend on Him each step of the way.

RESPOND

Who are the people you see every day as you travel the same streets, roads, stores, and hallways? Do you really "see" them or have you lost notice of them? Do you see them as immoveable objects or as people with stories and dreams? Make note of some people you used to notice but don't pay much attention to anymore.

Ask God to give you one person, just one, to see this week. Ask Him to give you eyes to notice someone who has been otherwise overlooked.

Once found, begin to pray for that person. Ask God for the grace and courage to not only see that person, but to stop and come alongside him or her. Ask God for insight to love that person out of the natural overflow of His love in you.

RECEIVE

_____, as you see, stop, and spend time with others, know that "my grace is sufficient for you, for my power is made perfect in weakness. Know that in your weakness, I am strong." (2 Corinthians 12:9-10)

DAY 35
WALKING WITH, NOT JUST WORKING FOR, GOD

As God's love in us grows, so does the temptation to make His love about our work and not our work about His love. True intimacy with God pushes us further into God-dependence and away from self-dependence. Satan relishes the opportunity to convince us otherwise.

RE-POSITION

Changing our posture of prayer can not only change the way we pray, it can move our outlook, attitude, and focus in a whole new direction. Try this posture of prayer: outstretch your arms toward the heavens and lift your head high as well. With this posture of welcome, openness, vulnerability, and awareness that there are things much bigger and higher than you, glorify and praise God. Acknowledge His greatness, power, and love. Express to Him with words, shouts, or even with silence, whatever is on your heart and mind. Ask Him to meet you where you are with whatever He knows you need.

RENEW

Consider the following passage adapted from a familiar story in Luke 10. Insert your own name in the passage (Luke 10:40-42) and see if God reveals any truth to you in the matter.

But _____ was distracted by all the preparations that had to be made. Coming to Jesus, _____ asked, "Lord, don't you care that I have been left to do all the work by myself? Tell someone to help me!"

"_____, _____," the Lord answered, "you are worried and upset about many things, but few things are needed – or indeed only one. Choose what is better, and it will not be taken away from you."

Now reflect a few moments on the verse below.

I am the vine; you are the branches. If you remain in me and I in you, you will bear much fruit; apart from me you can do nothing. (John 15:5)

FOOD FOR THOUGHT AND REFLECTION

Long before the first Star Trek "Vulcan salute" by Mr. Spock in 1967, people everywhere have yearned to "live long and prosper." Something within each of us desires for our lives to matter, to make a difference, to impact others far beyond our own realms of influence and lifespan. Whether or not we can readily articulate it, what we really want is for our lives to have "weight," or as the Scriptures describe it, "to be glorious."

We want our lives to matter, because we were created for such. As the loving creation of an all-glorious God, our lives are meant to bear fruit "worth their weight in gold" ... and glory.

The question has never been, "Am I meant to bear fruit that matters?" The real question is, "How do I go about bearing authentic, worthwhile, glorious fruit that honors God?" Unfortunately, far too many followers of Jesus have tried to bear fruit in a most unfruitful way. For many, the energy and effort they expend in the scurried activities of trying to "do what Jesus did" most often leaves them worn out, dried up, and done in. They end up working for Jesus without really walking with Him. As Dallas Willard says, "Spirituality wrongly understood or pursued is a major source of human misery and rebellion against God." No wonder so many feel so distant from God.

The solution, then, is not to try harder but to go deeper. The deeper we go in intimacy with God, the more we will bear relevant and meaningful life-fruit. Our call is to downward mobility. As we decrease, God's love in and through us increases. Jesus said it this way, "Unless a kernel of wheat falls to the ground and dies, it remains only a single seed. But if it dies, it produces many seeds" (John 12:24).

So, don't try harder, go deeper. "As you abide in me," Jesus says, "you will bear much fruit" (John 15:5).

RESPOND

Here are some questions for you to ponder and discuss with Jesus:

Are you tired and weary from life and ministry? If so, why do you think that is?

Is God the one asking you to do all that is currently on your plate or are you trying to please someone else or satisfy some other motive or need at work in you?

Do you ever feel like, "If anything is ever going to get done around here, I guess I'll have to do it?" If so, do you think that line of reasoning is healthy to your soul?

Outside of this devotional journey, when's the last time you spent quality time with Jesus and, as one song writer describes, got "lost in wonder, love, and praise"?

What do you think about this statement: "We weren't created to be human doings but human beings?"

RECEIVE

_____, Are you tired? Worn out? Burned out on religion? Come to me. Get away with me and you'll recover your life. I'll show you how to take a real rest. Walk with me and work with me — watch how I do it. Learn the unforced rhythms of grace. I won't lay anything heavy or ill-fitting on you. Keep company with me and you'll learn to live freely and lightly.
(Matthew 11:28-30, The Message)

WEEK 6
Maturing in Love

Some things were just meant to get better with time.
Love is one of them.
Time alone will not make your love better;
however, careful attention to giving yourself
to God over time will.
A steady, obedient love becomes one
that is true and deep,
whose roots become as the mighty oak,
and whose fruit abundantly multiplies.

DAY 36
MATURING IN LOVE THROUGH A RHYTHMIC LIFE

Life consists of a series of moments and events both monumental and mundane. "To everything there is a time and season," the writer of Ecclesiastes tells us; and moving to a rhythm of God with-ness sustains and deepens love through it all.

RE-POSITION

Nothing in life that we engage in is more rhythmic than our heart beating and our lungs breathing. In fact, irregular rhythms of heart and chest, arrhythmia, is not only dangerous to our health, it can be fatal. Take some time to slow down, way down, and actually listen for the beating of your heart and the intake and outflow of your breath. Put your hand on your chest for a few moments. Cup your hand gently over your mouth. Listen. Feel. Think. If you're like most, you simply take heartbeats, breath, and rhythm for granted. Choose not to do that today. Give God thanks for blood, and air, and syncopated tempos that give and sustain life.

RENEW

Think about all the rhythms God has created. Days and nights, months and years, seasons and ocean tides, breath and pulse, meters and cadences in music, dance, speech, and writing. The list is somewhat endless. Circle the words "pants" and "thirsts" in the passage below. As you meditate on the following verses, what do you hear God saying about how natural and rhythmic our love and dependence on Him is or should be?

As the deer pants for streams of water, so my soul pants for you, my God. My soul thirsts for God, for the living God. (Psalm 42:1-2)

FOOD FOR THOUGHT AND REFLECTION

Creating routines in our lives is a challenge, to say the least. It seems so often that everything schedules our schedules. Life comes too hard and too fast. But it is possible to grab the reigns and pace ourselves in a manner that can provide steady rhythms in every realm of life.

In ancient Jewish culture, the week rotated around the Sabbath, and the seasons were marked by feasts and festivals. While some traditions utilize a Sabbath day (a broader time span than what Sunday's have become) and various feasts, it is certainly not commonplace. We may also think that we do set certain times of the calendar year around holy days (such as Christmas and Easter), and there is a fuller expanse of the Christian calendar available that is utilized in some segments of the Church (including the seasons of Advent, Epiphany, Pentecost, Lent, along with Christmas and Easter). All in all, however, we are not very familiar with having our clocks and calendars set by God's time as opposed to the over-familiarity of pressing too many things into each day.

In short, allowing our faith story to mature by way of a rhythmic life will unfold if we decide to set boundaries, saying yes to what is needful and saying no to what is not needful. Planning weekly Sabbath—a time of really resting, recreating, and remembering who we are and who God is—sets the tone not only for the rest of the days of the week, it creates a space where we can begin to discern what are the most valuable things to incorporate into a healthy rhythm of life.

There are things in life that are simply beyond our control. There are also things that we can place into order, not for rigidity and legalistic purposes, but for the purpose of freedom.

RESPOND

Think about how naturally a deer living in the midst of forest and mountain pants for water. Imagine all the needed running and leaping, the unpredictability of weather, the presence of predators, and the need for daily sustenance just to survive. In the midst of all the up and down changes a deer experiences on a daily basis, he never seems to forget how to be thirsty or where to go for water. What are your "go-to" rhythms that keep you sane and sustained no matter what is occurring amid all the variables of your life? If you aren't sure what those rhythms are or might be, ask God to help you discover them.

How are you doing with the rhythmic gift God provided from the beginning in taking Sabbath? Be sure not to think in legalistic terms here. This means much more than just going to church on Sunday. Sabbath is God's gift of a seven day cycle whereby you remember that you were made for life and freedom in Him, not work and slavery from the hands of others. It includes all kinds of forms of resting, relaxing, rejoicing, remembering, relating, recreating, renewing ... just to name a few. If you haven't really trusted God with Sabbath or taken advantage of His gift, ask God how to go about changing that.

Write down what you hear Him saying ...

RECEIVE

_____, by day I direct my love toward you, at night my song is with you. (Psalm 42:8)

MATURING IN LOVE THROUGH SPIRITUAL DISCIPLINES

While a journey of a thousand miles begins with a single step, it's the intentional plodding of the other nine hundred and ninety-nine steps that helps you arrive at the destination. Love is a choice. Daily choosing to engage in ways that will deepen your love with God will, as Robert Frost put it, "make all the difference" as you choose the harder but better road.

RE-POSITION

An overlooked spiritual discipline these days is fasting. Fasting takes on many forms beyond the denial of food. You can abstain from a whole host of things—from sports to shopping to internet or cell usage. The point of fasting is to create spaces and appetites that drive you to depend on God to satisfy your deepest longings and needs.

Take the next 3-5 minutes to practice fasting from words. Fast, not just from spoken words, but thought ones as well. That means no conversations in your head, no speaking to God in prayer, no commenting internally on this or that. We speak so much more than we listen. Fasting from words will help you to better hear God and what He has to say. This fast may prove more difficult than first imagined. That's okay. God loves when we want to please Him by thinking more of Him and His ways than our own. Your desire to please Him will, in fact, please Him—no matter how well you pull off this spiritual discipline.

RENEW

Continue your practice of listening. Read the following passage two times. Read carefully and intentionally, taking time to pause after each reading in order that God's Word might wash over and cover you. Listen. Then listen some more. If you hear God speaking, write down whatever you hear.

Do you not know that in a race all the runners run, but only one gets the prize? Run in such a way as to get the prize. Everyone who competes in the games goes into strict training. They do it to get a crown that will not last, but we do it to get a crown that will last forever. Therefore I do not run like someone running aimlessly; I do not fight like a boxer beating the air. No, I strike a blow to my body and make it my slave so that after I have preached to others, I myself will not be disqualified for the prize. (1 Corinthians 9:24-27)

FOOD FOR THOUGHT AND REFLECTION

We don't really like the word "discipline." It means, well, it means that something requires discipline, training, hard work, decisive steps toward a goal. Much like choosing to set boundaries for a rhythmic life, spiritual disciplines bring us more freedom and more vitality. In spite of the negative connotations the word and the practice brings, it is necessary we implement— discipline.

A running theme throughout this 40-day awakening invitation is choosing to engage and entering the story right where you, are with what you have. Walking forward toward greater maturity is indicative of continuing to choose spiritual disciplines.

Primarily, *prayer* and *study* will fuel us. However, there are a host of practices that will also fan the flame of growing intimacy with God.

Fasting. Abstaining from food for two meals one day a week. Turning off social media and other electronic communications for a day, a week, or a month.

Solitude. Creating space on a monthly basis where you unplug and retreat for 24 hours. Being still, being quiet, not talking. Learning to be alone with God and your own thoughts.

Community. Purposefully involving yourself with the Body of Christ. Stepping out of comfort zones, knowing others, and allowing others to know you.

Physical exercise. Training our bodies helps to foster clearer thinking, emotional wholeness, and improved physical functioning.

Rest. Revisit Day 36 regarding rhythmic living. Allowing our bodies and minds to rest in a routine fashion, both in a daily pattern of retiring and rising, as well as extended periods of resting and replenishing.

Recreation. Play is so critical to our health and wholeness—spiritually, physically, and emotionally. The discipline of play is as important to adults as to young children.

Service. Living outside of ourselves and outside of our regular bubbles of routine and community lends to an expansion of seeing the world with God's eyes, to increasing our heart capacity for a world in need of the hope of Christ.

Maturing still takes discipline. It's worth every bit of tenacity it takes to live it.

RESPOND

For each of the spiritual disciplines listed, ask God if there is something He would like you to be doing in that area. If there is, write it down … and then do it! You may want to ask someone reliable (and lovingly firm) to keep you honest about doing what you alone committed to do. If you don't hear God speaking about a particular area, feel free to skip it. The goal of spiritual disciplines is not to be super-spiritual, it's to grasp hold of knowing, loving, and serving Jesus in profound, life-giving and Kingdom-impacting ways. This list isn't exhaustive, so by all means, add to and alter it however is helpful to you.

Prayer	Physical exercise
Study	Rest
Fasting	Recreation
Solitude	Community
Service	_____

RECEIVE

_____, you have faith pioneers who blazed the way, and they're cheering you on. That being so, it's time to get on with it. Strip down, start running — and never quit! No extra spiritual fat, no parasitic sins. Keep your eyes on Jesus, who both began and finished this race we're in. Study how he did it. Because he never lost sight of where he was headed — that exhilarating finish in and with God — he could put up with anything along the way: Cross, shame, whatever. And now he's there, in the place of honor, right alongside God. When you find yourselves flagging in your faith, go over that story again, item by item, that long litany of hostility he plowed through. That will shoot adrenaline into your souls! (Hebrews 12:1-3, The Message, adapted)

DAY 38

MATURING IN LOVE THROUGH DATES WITH GOD

Let the reality of this truth settle in: God actually wants to spend time with you! In fact, He delights in the thought of a "He and you" and "you and Him" encounter. What better way for love to flourish than prolonged times of cherished engagement.

RE-POSITION

Lamentations 3:22-23 tells us that "the steadfast love of the Lord never ceases; his mercies never come to an end; they are new every morning." That truth inspired one of the great hymns of the church, "Great Is Thy Faithfulness." Sing a hymn or song of praise to God today. Whether you sing the lyrics below or another song of your own choosing, let God know how much you really think of Him by expressing your praise and love through song. Let loose. Let your voice fill the air around you with unadulterated praise.

> *Great is Thy faithfulness, O God my Father;*
> *There is no shadow of turning with Thee;*
> *Thou changest not, Thy compassions, they fail not;*
> *As Thou hast been, Thou forever will be.*
> *Great is Thy faithfulness!*
> *Great is Thy faithfulness!*
> *Morning by morning new mercies I see.*
> *All I have needed Thy hand hath provided;*
> *Great is Thy faithfulness, Lord, unto me!*

"Great Is Thy Faithfulness" Words by: Thomas O. Chisholm (1923), Music by: William M. Runyon

RENEW

Martin Luther once said, "I have so much to do that I shall spend the first three hours in prayer." He wasn't alone. He followed the lead of Jesus who was often surrounded by human need but found life too busy not to pray. Prayer became the center by which all His other activity became meaningful, strength-filled, and prioritized. After carefully reading the passage below, ask Jesus, "Why was it you often got away and spent time with the Father?" If you're having a hard time hearing, read the entire chapter of Luke 5 for more insight.

Yet the news about [Jesus] spread all the more, so that crowds of people came to hear him and to be healed of their sicknesses. But Jesus often withdrew to lonely places and prayed. (Luke 5:15-16)

FOOD FOR THOUGHT AND REFLECTION

A love that grows is a love that is watered. Without intentional care, love becomes dry and lifeless. Most of us would never consider an "I do" at the altar to be enough for a marriage to last for a lifetime. Still, many of us have seen way too many marriages where "the light's on, but nobody is home." Friendships are the same way. Not many would expect a friendship to flourish simply by an occasional email, text, or tweet. Contact like that doesn't grow relationships—at best, it maintains them. Most of us want more than that in our human relationships, and we certainly need more than that in our relationship with the living God. He made us for abiding fruitfulness with Him, not some kind of appeasing relationship that just gets by.

Because love and relationships are as real and organic as plants, flowers, trees, or any other living and growing thing, we must give them "on purpose" care and attention. Amazingly, when we do, they really do grow. And while growth isn't always fun and happy, a healthy kind of growth is always beneficial in producing a deeper kind of love in us and through us that brings glory to God and fulfillment to our souls.

That's why Jesus, "as often as possible, withdrew to out-of-the-way places for prayer" (Luke 5:16, The Message). He wanted to connect with His Father in deeper, more meaningful ways. Jesus' times away with God were filled with all kinds of heart to heart conversation—thankfulness, delight, agony, discernment, suffering, and joy. Does this sound like some of the content that fills your heart? God longs for the space and time to connect with you in deeper ways as well—to hear your heart and to share His heart with you. Will you let Him?

RESPOND

Imagine God calls you and asks you to spend an afternoon with Him in the next month or so. He says He really loves your company and He would love to have some undivided, uninterrupted time alone with you ... just because. Would you say "yes"? If, in all honesty, you'd say "no," what would be the reason you'd give Him as to why you couldn't or wouldn't? Write it here.

Truthfully, God is calling, and He does want a date with you. If your heart says "yes," get your calendar out and pen in a time to have a Date Alone With God (D.A.W.G.). Protect the time you choose as you would any other important event in your life.

RECEIVE

You have been privileged to receive God's blessing day after day. Today, bless God as you go:

You, God, are my God, earnestly I seek you;
I thirst for you, my whole being longs for you in a dry and parched
land where there is no water.
I have seen you in the sanctuary
and beheld your power and your glory.
Because your love is better than life, my lips will glorify you.
I will praise you as long as I live,
and in your name I will lift up my hands.

(Psalm 63:1-4)

MATURING IN LOVE THROUGH BELIEF AND DEPENDENCE

While not believing God and depending on yourself will create distance between you and God quicker than anything, believing God and depending on Him deepens your love and faith like nothing else.

RE-POSITION

The downfall of Adam and Eve in the garden began by entertaining the serpent's question, "Did God really say …?" (Genesis 3:3). We would avoid a lot of ruin and draw closer to God in a much more intimate way if we would simply go directly to God with our questions. As you begin today, have a conversation with God. Share with Him some questions you may be struggling with or having difficulty understanding. Ask Him to teach you what is true, good, and right—even if that means it takes awhile for the answer. Express to God your willingness to trust Him in the absence of evident answers or direction.

RENEW

As you study the passage below, underline or circle the certain tasks that belong to God and the other responsibilities that belong to you. What are you to do and not do? And what are the rewards and benefits that come about when you do your part and God does His?

Trust in the Lord with all your heart, and lean not on your own understanding; in all your ways submit to him, and he will make your paths straight.
(Proverbs 3:5-6 NIV)

Trust God from the bottom of your heart; don't try to figure out everything on your own. (Proverbs 3:5-6 The Message)

Listen for God's voice in everything you do, everywhere you go; He's the One who will keep you on track.

FOOD FOR THOUGHT AND REFLECTION

Wouldn't it be great if life just always made sense, the direction was always clear, and everyone just always got along? Within each of us lies a sense that life is somehow supposed to be that way. At the same time, however, if we remain alert to the realities in us and all around us, we know life just isn't so. Somewhere trapped between the Garden of Eden and the Garden of Paradise we live in a broken world where hurt people hurt other hurting people. And in the end, who can you really trust and rely on? Our tendency, especially in the unclear and uncertain times, is to keep our lives close to our chest, controlling what we can and depending on ourselves to see us through.

There will be times, no matter how deep your love for God, that the way will be unclear and uncertain. Jesus' promise is true, "in this world you will have much trouble" (John 16:33). Others will hurt you and turn from you. God may seem distant and far from you. And in such times, you will be tempted to lean on your own strength and understanding. And if you do, you will make a mess of things and your love relationship with God and others will suffer.

Whether in the daily routines of life or in the midst of our darkest trials, we have two choices: run to God or run from Him, walk with Him or go it alone. Our love deepens when we lay our desire to understand and control things at the feet of the One who has overcome the world. In all your ways, in every situation, lean in and on God, and in His timing and plan, "he will direct your path" in a clear and loving way (Proverbs 3:5-6). As your trust and dependence on Him through the easy and hard places of life increases, so will your love.

RESPOND

Do some heart and soul searching. Be as honest with God as you know how to be. Where are some places you are, or have been, "leaning on your own understanding"? Confess to the Lord your unbelief: "Lord, forgive me for not believing that …"

Where are the places you have been, or are, depending on your own knowledge, strength, and resources? Take some time to bring each of those to the Lord as well. Ask Him to forgive you for taking things into your own hands. Ask Him for grace, courage and patience to trust and depend on Him more.

RECEIVE

_____, If you love me, keep my commands. And I will ask the Father, and he will give you another advocate to help you and be with you forever – the Spirit of truth. The world cannot accept him, because it neither sees him nor knows him. But you know him, for he lives with you and will be in you. I will not leave you as an orphan, _____; I will come to you. Before long, the world will not see me anymore, but you will see me. Because I live, you also will live, _____. On that day you will realize that I am in my Father, and you are in me, and I am in you. (John 14:15-20)

MATURING IN LOVE THROUGH A LONG OBEDIENCE IN THE SAME DIRECTION

Steady wins the race. You will go through seasons of being on the right track and feeling close to God; and in other seasons, you will feel like you've failed and God seems distant and silent. Much like marriage, your relationship with God is a long series of choices and events that are for better and worse, richer and poorer, and ailing and healthy, where a daily "I choose you" wins the day and sees you across the finish line.

RE-POSITION

Clear the table or area in front of you. Look around you and pick some objects that represent some of the things that are on your heart and mind. They could be good things, happy things, struggling things, stressful things, sad things, or hopeful things. You get the idea. Whatever they are, put them on the table or in front of you and tell God why you picked the things you did. Thank the Lord for meeting you just as you are, wherever you are.

RENEW

Jesus often spoke in stories, called parables. While stories have many sides and angles, parables have a single point or punch line. After you read the following passage, ask the Lord, "what is it you want me to know as I read this story you told long ago?"

He also said, "This is what the kingdom of God is like. A man scatters seed on the ground. Night and day, whether he sleeps or gets up, the seed sprouts and grows, though he does not know how. All by itself the soil produces grain — first the stalk, then the head, then the full kernel in the head. As soon as the grain is ripe, he puts the sickle to it, because the harvest has come."
(Mark 4:26-29)

FOOD FOR THOUGHT AND REFLECTION

Some things, like wine and cheese, just get better with time. It's not just the passing of time, however, that make such things better. It's a submission to a certain set of practices over a long period of time that actually does the trick. Such variables as room temperature, humidity, and proper rotation go into making things like wine and cheese better over time. Putting in the time alone doesn't make things tastier. What gives wine and cheese exquisite flavor is the right care, in the right place, for the right amount of time.

And so it is with your love relationship with God. Just putting in the time with God won't make your intimacy with Him grow. Knowing the number of days since you committed your life to Christ won't draw you closer to Him. Neither will showing up weekly for church, having a daily Bible reading plan, doing devotions, feeding the homeless, or praying at meals and bedtime. These are good things. Needed things. But, unless these spiritual practices (along with any others) are done with a heart that longs to know God and do what He says, they become no more than a ticking of the clock without beneficial purpose.

Your love and intimacy with God, however, is meant for maturing, sweetening, and deepening. And that will happen when you "seek him with your whole heart" (Jeremiah 29:13), meet Him in the places and spaces He provides through spiritual practices and disciplines, and learn to hear and respond obediently and quickly to God's voice. The right heart combined with the right practices, over time, will deepen your love with God as you together navigate the up and down, peaks and valleys, rough and plain places of life. And as you place the seeds of your love in God's rich Kingdom soil, over time, Jesus says, your love for Him will grow and ripen "all by itself" (Mark 4:28). May it be so!

RESPOND

Jesus loved to tell stories. Today, He'd love to hear yours. Take some time to write your story. While Jesus knows your story far better than you do, He delights to hear you tell it. The beauty of your story is that it is yours! Even more beautiful is the fact God continues to write your love story as a part of His epic narrative titled, "I'm Making All Things New!"

As you look at your love adventure ahead, express to God the places you long to go. Share with Him any fears or hesitancies you might face in going. Finally, give Him thanks for the great love story He is continuing to write in you and in others.

RECEIVE

_____, as the Father has loved me, so have I loved you. Now remain in my love. If you keep my commands, you will remain in my love, just as I have kept my Father's commands and remain in his love. I have told you this so that my joy may be in you and that your joy may be complete. (John 15:9-11)

And now, as you continue in your journey of love, _____,

> *May the Lord bless you and keep you.*
> *May the Lord make His face to shine upon you,*
> *and be gracious to you.*
> *May the Lord lift up His countenance upon you,*
> *and give you peace. Amen.*

Conclusion

Congratulations! Unless you are just one of those people who like to eat dessert before dinner begins or read the last chapter of a book first in order to sneak a peek at how the story ends, you have most likely just finished a diligently paced, 40-day journey with God. Well done!

And that is the hope, isn't it? To hear the One who calls you "beloved" say with great delight, "Well done!"

You gave it all you had and kept on bringing it—"Well done!"

You grasped hold of the fact that I am *really* yours and you are *really* Mine— "Well done!"

You are really beginning to see that love is so much more about right heart motive than right conduct—"Well done!"

You have stepped further into the fellowship and unity of Father, Son, and Holy Spirit as you have pursued Me with your whole heart—"Well done!"

"Well done, good and faithful servant. Come and share in my joy and happiness" (Matthew 25:23).

Well done, indeed! What a great beginning! And that is exactly what this is—a beginning. No matter how long any of us have walked with God, our most sacred moments and spiritually locked-in seasons still only scratch the surface of God's inexhaustible love.

But don't let that disparity discourage you in any way, because the best is yet to come! As you continue to abide in Christ, and He in you, your love will only get stronger, sweeter, more faithful and true.

While this 40-day journey may not have earned you a certificate or degree, our sincere hope has been that you have come away with something much greater: a deeper love encounter with Jesus Himself. Our prayer is that you continue to know Him in authentic and unmistakable ways as you walk and talk, listen and reflect, move and respond, and rest and rejoice with Him.

God is not a book to be finished or a course to be completed. There is profound beauty and wonder in never quite figuring out the fullness of God. You are satisfied, yet you long for more. You are filled to overflowing, yet you continually yearn for more. That is what Jesus was talking about in the beatitudes when He said, "blessed are you when you hunger and thirst for righteousness" (Matthew 5:6).

Have you ever met a couple that has been married fifty or sixty years, and they still have that glimmering twinkle in their eye? It is beautiful to behold. Certainly in that amount of time, hardships, unforeseen challenges, misunderstandings, and even doubts have tested the limits of their love. Yet, the glimmer remains. Why? Perhaps it is because, that even after six decades of doing life together, they have only begun to discover the depth, beauty, and wonder of one another. Every year is a new discovery of "I didn't know you liked that" or "You look more radiant than I've ever seen you." It is a marvelous mystery!

How much more the mystery of knowing and loving God! How high are the heavens with His love, how deep the ocean of His mercy, how wide His wisdom, how far-reaching His grace. What an indescribable treasure God is, a treasure to be opened, explored, discovered, savored, cherished. And, to add even more to this gift, He looks upon us and loves us as a treasure, to be opened, explored, discovered, savored, cherished. A profound mystery indeed!

May God's mysterious, yet ever-available love continue to awaken His love in you. May your heart, mind, body, and soul be forever stirred by the One who is able to do immeasurably more than you could ever ask or imagine, according to His power that is at work within you (Ephesians 3:20). May you always have ears that hear the Beloved One say:

"I have loved you with an everlasting love. Come, arise, and go with me. I am yours and you are mine." (Jeremiah 31:3, Song of Solomon 2:10, 6:3)

Next Steps

If God has renewed your mind, stirred your heart, and quickened your soul through this 40-day experience, chances are you will want to continue what God so lovingly began. You actually have all the tools you need to maintain a healthy and growing love relationship with Him. Your desire to genuinely please Him and your intentionality in practicing the Kingdom values and spiritual disciplines experienced in this guide will lead you well as you trust God to mature your life and love. With tools already in hand, here are three simple reminders to encourage you as you go:

Keep Abiding.

Keep after God. Don't stop. "As the Father has loved me, so have I loved you. Now remain in my love," John 15:9 tells us. You don't need this guide or any other devotional resource to pursue God with reckless abandon. Don't let Satan tell you otherwise. What you need is God Himself. Let the real God meet the real you. Showing up really is half the battle. Since you've started a great rhythm of meeting intimately with God over the last several weeks, be intentional and keep on going.

Keep Believing.

God is faithful and He keeps His promises. The apostle Paul assures us that "He who began a good work in you will be faithful to complete it" (Philippians 1:6). Life may be unpredictable and unknown. You may be equally the same. Regardless of the changing circumstances around you or the swirling feelings within you, God is constant and true, and He can be trusted. Learn to trust God in the unknown, unseen, unexpected, and unpredicted places. Practice trusting God, and see how big He really is!

Keep Company.

Traveling alone can be wearisome and dangerous. There's strength in numbers. "A cord of three strands is not quickly broken," Ecclesiastes 4:12 proclaims. Make sure you are running this race with others who want nothing more than to please God and serve His Kingdom. Life is too hard and the evil one too crafty for any of us to find much success going it alone. Find a church, a small group, a mentor, a spouse, a parent, a brother or sister, or a friend—whomever God leads you to. Pray for one another, encourage one another, study God's Word together, and live honestly together. Real people, with real struggles, and real big hearts to love and please God make the best traveling buddies. Ask God to lead you to one.

Dates, DAWGs, and Quick Connections

Here are some additional tips and suggestions for getting the most out of a 5-minute or a 5-hour encounter with God. Whether on your commute to work, settling into an established devotional time, or spending extended time alone with God, these practices should prove helpful in conversation and engagement. The only significant difference between a quick conversation with God and a weekend away with Him is the length of time you devote to each portion of your encounter.

RE-POSITION

Shifting from craziness to solitude takes some re-positioning of body, mind, and spirit. Here's some guidance on how to do just that:

Resist

Avoid making this "the perfect time with God." Don't waste time on trivial things like the perfect location, music, phone calls, etc. God wants to meet you. Satan wants to distract you.

Relocate

Find a comfortable place away from the things that distract you. For some, that may be a single place, for others it may be several places as you walk and talk with God. Do what fits you. Decide this way, "Where can Jesus and I talk personally for awhile?"

Relax

Slow waaaay down. Begin to listen to yourself breathe. Close your eyes and picture Jesus with you (because He is!). Ask God to release any tension you may be feeling in your body, mind, or spirit. "Breathe in" God's peace.

Release

"Exhale" the worries, thoughts, cares, and tasks that enter your mind … acknowledge them and then release them to God. Ask God to keep you from being pre-occupied by them. If it's helpful, write your concerns on a list that you can return to later.

Rest

Rest is sometimes the holiest thing you can do. Take a short nap if needed. Thank God for resting with you and for making you more alive and alert.

Remember

Recall God's goodness and work in your life and in the world. Thank Him for what has been—the good and the bad, the smooth and the rough, the clear and the confusing.

Rejoice

Praise God with all you have and are. "Let all that is within you bless the Lord" (Ps 103, 105)—use speech, pen, music, song, dance, or any other loving expression you can think of … whatever means you choose, let it out!

RENEW

Here are a few ways God may want to connect with you and deepen your love:

Simply be quiet and listen to God intently • Meditate on a few verses or a whole passage of Scripture • Take a walk with God • Read a book • Doodle, sketch, or diagram whatever comes to mind • Ask God questions • Listen and make lists • View your surroundings, tell God what you see — ask Him what He sees • Exercise or creatively design something and allow God to speak • Dream out loud • Sing songs and see where God takes you • Write God a letter and wait for His response

Not sure where to start? Pick something and begin. God honors movement. He will lead you from there.

RESPOND

Here are some ways you may want to respond as you encounter God.

Give thanks. Express your gratitude to God for His renewing work in you.

Get it out, get it down. Whether journaling, drawing, creating, recording, speaking, etc.—through a means and medium that fits you, express things like: "What all just took place here?" "What I really want to say to you God is ..." "Lord, some things I hear you saying to me are ..." "Some questions I have are ..." and, of course, anything else on your heart and mind. Let it flow!

Next steps. Reflect on what you may need to do in response to your time together with God. Do I need to share some of this with a trusted friend? Do I need to ask someone's forgiveness? Do I need to lay something down or pick something up? Do I need some guided help beyond my own ability to deal with things? Do I need to keep listening or wait for further instructions? Whatever God is saying, write it down, and put some kind of date/time beside it as to when you will act on it.

RECEIVE

You may want to simply open your hands, listen, and receive. Equally, here are some Scripture passages that you can personalize as God's Word puts voice to God's promises and blessing to you. However you choose to listen and receive, don't rush. Let the real God meet the real you!

Jn 14:27	Jer 29:11-13	Rom 8:28
I Pet 5:10	2 Cor 5:17	Ps 27:1
Isa 40:29-31	Mt 11:28	I Pet 5:10
Phil 4 6-9	Deut 31:6	2 Cor 12:9
Ps 32:8	Isa 41:10	Lk 3:22
Rom 8:37-39	Phil 4:19	Acts 1:8
2 Thes 2:16-17	Ps 103:11-12	Num 6:24-26

Additional Resources

Written and Audio Resources

(ForgeForward.org/Resources)

- *Forged by Fire* by Dwight Robertson with John Boyd

- *Is God Waiting for a Date with You?* by Dwight Robertson

- *You Are God's Plan A* by Dwight Robertson (book and study guide)

- "Two Wings that Soar: The Power of Praise and Prayer" audio recording by Dwight Robertson

More Fuel

(ForgeForward.org)

- Forge Blog: *ForgeForward.org/Blog*

- Forge Prayer Team: *ForgeForward.org/Prayer*

- "Forge Spark of the Day"—a daily text to challenge and encourage (text SPARK to 33222 to subscribe)

- "Date Alone With God 101": *ForgeForward.org/DAWG*

Training and Growth Opportunities for All Ages

(ForgeForward.org/Equipping)

- The Experience

- Surge

- Deep Camp

- DAWGs and WAAWGs for individuals and couples

- Life Planning

Awakening